TART
IT UP!

SWEET & SAVORY
TARTS & PIES

Eric Lanlard

Photography by Kate Whitaker

TART
IT UP!

SWEET & SAVORY
TARTS & PIES

Eric Lanlard

Photography by Kate Whitaker

Mitchell Beazley

Contents

Sweet Tarts and Pies 96

Recipes:

Quick sweet bakes 164

Sweet accompaniments 167

Introduction

I will always remember the morning I walked into the pastry kitchen of Le Grand Pâtisserie in Quimper, France, for the first time ... I was petrified, but excited, and could not wait to start learning how to make all the wonderful creations I had been dreaming of since I was a young kid. I confidently expected that I would begin by making a glamorous celebration or wedding cake, and was a bit disappointed to be told I would have to spend my first six months in the pastry section, making pastry day in, day out. Looking back, however, I understand how important these months were. Pastry making is a very intricate skill, and it doesn't matter how delicious the filling, fruit, or garnish is— if the pastry is not good, it will ruin the whole experience.

The following six months were spent learning how to use all the fabulous pastry that I now had at my fingertips—it was time to be creative and turn these tarts and pies into delicious works of art, using all the techniques, ingredients, and equipment at my disposal. I discovered that a good pâtissier was expected to be able to produce great savory items as well as sweet ones, and as a result my friends have been asking me for years to put down on paper some of my savory creations, which they've tasted during impromptu dinners and alfresco lunches at my house and which they love so much.

So ... voilà! In this new book, you will find not only great recipes and tips for making the best pastry but also the inspiration for delicious tarts and pies that I've collected over the years—classic ones that I've given my own twist, and new ones that I've created following ideas gleaned from my travels. I hope you will like them as much as my friends do.

Bisous,
Eric x

PASTRY BASICS

The addition of fresh or dried herbs and spices to the dough will give the piecrust a nice twist.

Flaky pastry dough

**Makes 14½ oz
or enough to line a 9 inch diameter,
1¼ inch deep tart pan**
Preparation time: 10 minutes, plus chilling

2 cups all-purpose flour, plus extra for dusting

1 teaspoon fine salt

1¼ sticks unsalted butter, chopped into pieces

1 egg, beaten

1 tablespoon milk

Sift the flour and salt into a large mixing bowl. Using your fingertips, rub in the butter until the mixture resembles fine bread crumbs.

Make a well in the center and add the rest of the ingredients. Again using your fingertips, mix together to make a smooth dough.

Turn the dough out onto a lightly floured surface and lightly knead two or three times. Cover with plastic wrap and chill for at least 30 minutes before using. See pages 18–19 for how to line a pan and prebake the crust.

Any leftover dough can be frozen for up to 6 weeks.

Variation

For whole-wheat pastry dough, follow the recipe above but reduce the amount of all-purpose flour to 1 cup and add 1 cup whole-wheat flour.

You can vary the flavor of this pastry dough by adding citrus rind, mint, or ground spices.

You can replace the ground almonds with other ground nuts, such as hazelnuts, walnuts, or pistachios.

Sweet flaky pastry dough

Makes 1lb
or enough to line a 10-inch diameter,
1¼ inch deep tart pan
Preparation time: 10 minutes, plus chilling

2 cups plus 6 tablespoons all-purpose flour, plus extra for dusting

4 tablespoons superfine sugar

1¾ sticks unsalted butter, chopped into pieces

2 egg yolks

2 tablespoons cold water

2 teaspoons vanilla paste or extract

Sift the flour into a large mixing bowl and stir in the sugar. Using your fingertips, rub in the butter until the mixture resembles bread crumbs.

Make a well in the center and add the rest of the ingredients. Again using your fingertips, mix together to make a smooth dough.

Turn out onto a lightly floured surface and gather together into a ball. Cover with plastic wrap and chill for at least 30 minutes before using. See pages 18–19 for how to line a pan and prebake the crust.

Any leftover dough can be frozen for up to 6 weeks.

Almond flaky pastry dough

Makes 1 lb 3½ oz
or enough to line 2 x 9 inch diameter,
1¼ inch deep tart pans
Preparation time: 10 minutes, plus chilling

¾ cup plus 1 tablespoon confectioners' sugar

1¼ sticks unsalted butter, chopped into pieces

½ cup ground almonds (almond meal)

½ teaspoon vanilla paste or extract

1–2 drops of almond extract

2 medium eggs, lightly beaten

1¾ cups plus 1 tablespoon all-purpose flour, plus extra for dusting

Sift the confectioners' sugar into a large bowl. Add the butter, ground almonds, vanilla paste, and almond extract, and rub together using your fingertips until the mixture resembles bread crumbs.

Stir in the eggs. Sift the flour and add to the mixture, then mix together using your fingertips or the blade of a knife. Turn onto a floured surface and form into a ball. Cover with plastic wrap and chill for at least 30 minutes before using. See pages 18–19 for how to line a pan and prebake the crust.

Any leftover dough can be frozen for up to 6 weeks.

I like to be sure that all elements of my recipes taste or complement each other and nothing works better than this rich dark chocolate pastry to match a chocolate-based creation.

Chocolate flaky pastry dough

**Makes 14½ oz
or enough to line a 9 inch diameter,
1¼ inch deep tart pan**
Preparation time: 10 minutes, plus chilling

1½ cups plus 2 tablespoons all-purpose flour,
plus extra for dusting

¼ cup plus 1 tablespoon unsweetened cocoa powder

⅓ cup plus 1 tablespoon confectioners' sugar

1¼ sticks unsalted butter, chopped into pieces

3 egg yolks

1 teaspoon vanilla paste or extract

Sift together the flour, cocoa, and confectioners' sugar into a large mixing bowl. Using your fingertips, rub in the butter until the mixture resembles bread crumbs.

Make a well in the center and add the egg yolks and vanilla. Again using your fingertips, mix together to make a smooth dough.

Turn the dough out onto a lightly floured surface and gather together into a ball. Cover with plastic wrap and chill for at least 30 minutes before using. See pages 18–19 for how to line a pan and prebake the crust.

Any leftover dough can be frozen for up to 6 weeks.

1

5

2

3

4

6

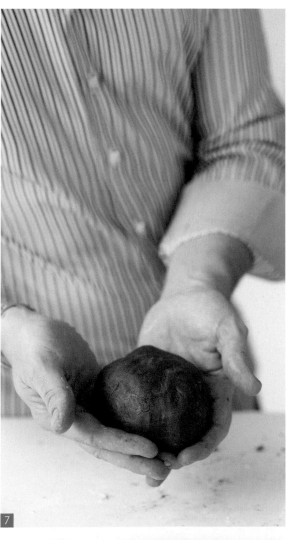

7

The light, buttery texture of this dough makes a great base for sweet and savory recipes. Any unused cooked pastry can be toasted to serve with pâté or buttered and drizzled with honey.

Brioche pastry dough

Makes 1 lb 13 oz

Preparation time: 10 minutes, plus kneading (25 minutes), rising (2 hours), and chilling (2 hours)

⅓ cup warm milk

1 (0.6 oz) fresh yeast cake or 1 (¼ oz) envelope active dry yeast

4 cups all-purpose flour, plus extra for dusting

1 teaspoon fine salt

6 eggs, beaten

3 sticks butter

2 tablespoons superfine sugar

Mix together the milk and fresh yeast. If using dry yeast, pour the milk into a bowl, sprinkle the yeast over it, and stir to blend. Let sit in a warm place for 15 minutes, or until the mixture becomes frothy.

Sift together the flour and salt. Using a freestanding electric mixer fitted with a dough hook, set the mixer on a low speed, add the flour and salt, then gradually add the yeast mixture to the flour with the eggs until blended. Knead for 5 minutes on a medium speed. Scrape down the sides using a spatula and knead at a faster speed for another 10 minutes, or until the dough almost stops sticking to the sides of the bowl.

Drop the speed to medium again, and add the butter and sugar, a little at a time until everything is incorporated. Increase to full speed and knead for 8–10 minutes, or until the dough is smooth and comes away from the sides of the bowl.

Place the dough in a large, lightly floured bowl and cover with plastic wrap. Let rise for 2 hours at room temperature—the dough should double in volume.

Knead the dough again, punching out all the air. Cover again and chill for 2 hours before using.

This is the king of pastries, and the flavor and texture when baked are worth all the effort. Any unused dough can be frozen for up to 6 weeks.

Puff pastry

Makes 2 lb

Preparation time: Chill overnight x 2, plus additional chilling time

3 cups plus 3 tablespoons all-purpose flour, plus extra for dusting

1–1½ teaspoons salt

6½ tablespoons cold unsalted butter, cut into small pieces

¾ cup plus 3 tablespoons cold water

2⅝ sticks unsalted butter, softened

1 extra-large egg yolk, beaten with 1 tablespoon milk, for an egg wash

Sift the flour and salt into a large bowl. Rub the cold cubes of butter into the flour, using your fingertips. Work quickly to keep the dough cold. It will be sticky. Make a well in the center and add all the water at once. Using a rubber spatula or your fingers, gradually draw the flour into the water. Mix until all the flour is incorporated. Do not knead.

Turn the dough out onto a lightly floured surface, and knead it a few times, rounding it into a ball. Wrap it in plastic wrap and chill overnight.

The dough and softened butter must be of equal consistency. If necessary, let the dough sit at room temperature to soften, or chill the butter to harden.

On a lightly floured board, roll the dough into a rectangle 12 x 15 inches. Using a pastry brush, remove any flour from the surface.

Position the block of butter in the center of the dough and press it down a little. Fold the four edges of the dough over the butter; stretch it, if necessary—none of the butter should be exposed. With the folded sides up, press the dough several times with a rolling pin; use a rocking motion to create ridges all over. Put the rolling pin in each ridge and slowly roll

to widen it. Repeat until all the ridges are doubled in size. Using the ridges as a starting point, roll the dough into a smooth, even rectangle 8 x 20 inches. Keep the corners of the dough as right angles. Fold the dough in thirds lengthwise, like a business letter. This completes the first turn. Rotate the dough 90 degrees so that the folded edge is on your left and the dough faces you like a book. Roll out again, repeating the ridging technique. Again, the dough should be in a smooth, even rectangle of 8 x 20 inches. Fold the dough in thirds again, completing the second turn. Cover the dough with plastic wrap and chill for at least 30 minutes.

Repeat the rotating, rolling, and folding until the dough has had five turns. Do not perform more than two turns without a resting and chilling period. Cover the dough and chill overnight before shaping and baking. Remember to chill after shaping for about 30 minutes before using.

To prebake, roll out until ⅛ inch thick, transfer to a nonstick baking sheet, prick all over with a fork, and brush with beaten egg. Bake in a preheated oven, at 400°F, for 15 minutes for individual tarts and 20 minutes for large tarts, or until golden. The timing may depend on the shape and size of the pastry.

Tips

Make sure you dust any loose flour away from the dough, because it can prevent the puff pastry from rising properly when baked.

Roll the dough without pushing too hard, otherwise you will break all the wonderful layers you made when creating the turns.

Puff pastry contains no egg or sugar, so it needs to be brushed with an egg wash before baking.

Lining a pan

Roll the dough out on a lightly floured surface or piece of plastic wrap to 2 inches larger than your pan.

Grease your pan, then lift the dough over a rolling pin and lightly drape it over the pan. For tarts, loose-bottom pans are best. Peel away the plastic wrap, if using.

Gently lift the edges of the dough upward and ease the dough into position. Press the dough firmly but gently into place with your fingertips, making sure that there are no gaps between the dough and the pan.

Turn any excess dough outward over the rim of the tart pan, then run the rolling pin over the top of the pan so that any excess dough is cut off. Smooth any rough edges with the side of a blunt knife.

Prebaking

Prebaking a pastry shell, sometimes referred to as "blind baking," refers to baking an empty pastry shell to make it firm, so that the filling doesn't make the piecrust soggy.

Prick the bottom of the pastry shell with a fork. Chill in the refrigerator for 15 minutes; this will help to stop it from shrinking during baking.

Place a large piece of nonstick parchment paper over the bottom and sides of the pastry shell. Fill the bottom with pie weights—these are available from the cookware department of large department stores and speciality cookware shops —or dried uncooked beans.

Bake in a preheated oven, at 350°F, for 10–15 minutes for a large tart or 8–10 minutes for individual tarts, or until the shell is just set, then remove the paper and weights and cook empty for another 10 minutes for a large tart or 4–5 minutes for individual tarts, or until the bottom is dry and crisp and the top edges of the tart are golden.

Leave the piecrust in the pan and continue with your chosen recipe.

5

SAVORY TARTS AND PIES

Savory

Savory tarts and pies have been dismissed in the past as heavy dishes only suitable for cold wintry weather or for casual snacks. Here, I'm demonstrating that savory tarts and pies can be baked right through the year, using seasonal ingredients and transforming them into gourmet dishes. As in the sweet chapter, I will show you that the use of new pastries, such a light buttery brioche, or the addition of herbs and nuts will elevate the standard of the most classic recipes. My love for the ingredients of the past is found here, too, with recipes using heirloom tomatoes or—one of my favorite—colorful heritage beets. At the same time, I'll show you how to make and rediscover true classics, such as Quiche Lorraine, in their full glory, made the way they should be.

Most of the inspiration for these chapters comes from memories of travel, family and friends, special occasions, or visits to fine eating establishments. I am sure these recipes will inspire you, too, and that you will discover a love of baking savory tarts and pies throughout the year.

This great spring tart looks and tastes like a morning walk through a beautiful vegetable garden. It is so fresh, and you can use whatever vegetable is in season in your vegetable plot or at the local farmers' market .

Spring garden green tart

Serves 6

Preparation time: 20 minutes, plus chilling

Cooking time: 50 minutes

butter, for greasing

all-purpose flour, for dusting

about ¾ quantity (11½ oz) flaky pastry dough (see page 10)

7 oz green asparagus, ends trimmed

½ cup fresh peas

½ cup fresh fava beans

3 eggs

⅓ cup Greek yogurt

¾ cup plus 2 tablespoons heavy cream

½ cup dry white wine

1 tablespoon fresh lemon thyme leaves

1 tablespoon snipped chives

1¼ cups freshly grated Parmesan cheese

salt and freshly ground black pepper

Butter a 10½ x 8 inch rectangular tart pan, 1¼ inches deep. Roll out the dough on a lightly floured surface and use it to line the pan. Lightly prick the bottom with a fork. Let rest in the refrigerator while preparing the filling.

Bring a saucepan of lightly salted water to a boil. Add the asparagus and cook for 5 minutes, or until cooked but still firm. Remove with a slotted spoon and refresh under cold running water. Repeat with the peas, cooking them for 3 minutes, then the fava beans, cooking them for 5 minutes.

Meanwhile, preheat the oven to 350°F.

Beat the eggs in a bowl and add the yogurt, cream, wine, and, finally, the fresh herbs. Beat well to blend, then season with salt and pepper.

Cover the bottom of the pastry shell with half the Parmesan and arrange the asparagus, peas, and beans over the top in an attractive way. Sprinkle over the rest of the Parmesan. Carefully pour the egg mixture over the vegetables—it should come right to the top. Bake in the oven for 30–35 minutes, or until set and golden.

At home, I serve this lovely tart with a celeriac rémoulade and a few thin slices of baked ham.

Tip

Always buy a block of Parmesan cheese and use it freshly grated.

The word "Mediterranean" says it all really—plump eggplant, colorful cherry tomatoes, anchovies, and capers, all cooked in a rich ricotta and cream filling.

Mediterranean tart

Serves 6

Preparation time: 25 minutes

Cooking time: 1 hour 35 minutes

For the pastry dough

2 cups all-purpose flour, plus extra for dusting

pinch of salt

1 stick unsalted butter, chilled and cubed, plus extra for greasing

1 egg yolk

2–3 tablespoons chilled water

For the filling

¼ cup olive oil

3 medium red onions, sliced

salt and freshly ground black pepper

1 large eggplant, cut into ½ inch slices

1 cup ricotta cheese

2 eggs, beaten

¼ cup heavy cream

5 oz halloumi cheese, thinly sliced, or 1 cup crumbled feta cheese

1 cup halved cherry tomatoes

6 anchovies, sliced lengthwise into thin strips

1 tablespoon capers, rinsed

fresh oregano leaves

To make the dough, put the flour and salt into a large bowl and rub in the chilled butter until the mixture resembles fine bread crumbs. Using a knife, mix in the egg yolk and then gradually add enough of the chilled water until the mixture comes together to form a dough—adding the water a little at a time will prevent the dough from becoming too sticky. Grease a 9 inch diameter, 1¼ inch deep tart pan, and line with the dough (see page 18). Chill in the refrigerator for 30 minutes.

Preheat the oven to 400°F. Remove the pastry shell from the refrigerator and prick the bottom with a fork. Line with wax paper and cover with pie weights or dried beans. Bake for 15 minutes, then remove the weights and paper and cook for another 10 minutes, or until golden.

Meanwhile to make the filling, heat half the olive oil in a heavy pan. Add the red onions, sprinkle with a little salt, and cook gently over low heat, stirring occasionally, until the onions release their natural sugars and begin to turn golden. This will take about 10–12 minutes.

Preheat the oven to 400°F. While the onions are cooking, brush the eggplant slices with the remaining olive oil and heat a ridged grill pan or skillet. Place the eggplants on the hot pan and cook until lightly browned on both sides. You may have to do this in batches.

Put the ricotta into a medium bowl and mix until smooth. Add the eggs and cream, and season with salt and pepper.

Cover the bottom of the cooked pastry shell with the softened onions and then overlap the slices of eggplant and the cheese on top. Cover this layer with the halved cherry tomatoes. Pour the ricotta and egg mixture over the vegetables and finally cover the top of the tart with the anchovies, capers, and a generous sprinkling of oregano leaves.

Return to the oven for 20–25 minutes, or until set and golden. Drizzle with olive oil before serving.

These little individual tarts are perfect as a light appetizer or to take on a picnic or outdoor meal. The long, slow cooking of the red onion produces a delightful sweet taste that is enhanced by the balsamic vinegar. The feta cheese and the partly baked tomatoes cut through the sweetness wonderfully.

Caramelized onion and feta tarts

Serves 6

Preparation time: 20 minutes

Cooking time: 1 hour

1⅓ cups halved cherry tomatoes

3 tablespoons extra virgin olive oil

1 garlic clove, finely chopped

2 tablespoons unsalted butter

5½ red onions (about 1¼ lb), thinly sliced

2 tablespoons balsamic vinegar

6 prebaked puff pastry shells, each 4 inch in diameter, using 10 oz store-bought or about ⅓ quantity homemade puff pastry (see page 16)

2 bunches of fresh wild arugula

1 cup crumbled feta cheese

salt and freshly ground black pepper

2 teaspoons oregano or thyme leaves, to garnish

Place the cherry tomatoes on a baking sheet, cut side facing up. Drizzle 1 tablespoon of the olive oil over them, then sprinkle with the garlic and season with salt and pepper.

Bake in a preheated oven, at 325°F, for 25 minutes, or until the tomatoes are nice and soft but not mushy. Remove from the oven, then increase the oven temperature to 350°F.

Meanwhile, caramelize the onions. Melt the butter in a saucepan with 1 tablespoon of the olive oil. Add the onions and cook gently over low heat for about 10–12 minutes, stirring continuously—this is a long process that will make the experience special. When the onions are caramelized but not brown (they should be dark pink), stir in the balsamic vinegar.

Divide the onions among the cooked pastry shells, then put them into the oven to reheat for 6 minutes.

Serve the tarts piled high with the arugula. Place a few warm roasted tomatoes around the edge and sprinkle the feta cheese generously on top. Drizzle with the remaining olive oil and garnish with chopped oregano or thyme leaves.

I fell in love with this traditional Moroccan recipe during my first visit to the Atlas Mountains. It was baked in a huge, outdoor wood oven and almost looked like a cake when it came out, but it was succulent and spicy. It is traditionally made with pigeon, but I like my version with chicken, because it is less dry.

Moroccan "pastilla" tart

Serves 8

Preparation time: 35 minutes

Cooking time: 1 hour

4 red onions (1 lb), finely chopped

1¾ sticks unsalted butter, plus extra for greasing

2 lb chicken pieces

bunch of fresh cilantro, coarsely chopped

2 tablespoons ground cinnamon

2 teaspoons ras el hanout

1 teaspoon saffron

1 tablespoon superfine sugar

¼ cup chicken or vegetable stock

1 lb brik pastry sheet or phyllo pastry sheets

1⅓ cups ground almonds (almond meal)

4 hard-boiled eggs, coarsely chopped

1 egg, lightly beaten

1 tablespoon confectioners' sugar, mixed with 1 teaspoon ground cinnamon

sea salt and freshly ground black pepper

In a large casserole dish, gently sauté the onions in half the butter over low heat for about 15 minutes. Add the chicken, cilantro, cinnamon, ras el hanout, saffron, and superfine sugar and season well with salt and pepper. Add the stock, cover the casserole, and cook over low heat for 20–25 minutes, stirring occasionally. Add more stock if it becomes too dry; however, the final mixture must be dry or the pastry will become soggy. Shred the chicken into ¾ inch pieces and put to one side to cool.

Preheat the oven to 375°F. Generously butter a 9 inch diameter, 1¼ inch deep tart pan.

Layer the sheets of pastry in the tart pan in a crisscross manner, making sure they overlap the edge of the pan and reserving 2 sheets for covering the top. Keep the sheets you are not using covered with a damp cloth to prevent them from drying out. Place a layer of the shredded chicken on top and sprinkle with some of the ground almonds and chopped eggs. Repeat the chicken, almond, and egg layers until they are all used.

Cut the remaining butter into small cubes and place them on top of the filling. Bring the overlapping pastry sides over the top of the tart and cover with the reserved sheets of pastry. Brush the top with the beaten egg. Bake in the oven for 25 minutes, or until the pastry is nice and golden.

Serve immediately with a generous dusting of confectioners' sugar and ground cinnamon. A fresh herb and arugula salad, dressed with balsamic vinegar, makes a nice light accompaniment.

Tip

Brik pastry is a Middle Eastern pastry used for both sweet and savory recipes. It is slightly thicker than phyllo pastry and is used in the same way. If you can't get hold of brik pastry use phyllo, but you might need an extra sheet to achieve the right thickness.

Memory lane it is, with this delicious recipe from my native Brittany. I suppose this used to be a way to use leftover seafood, but today it looks and tastes very sophisticated ... perfect for a main dish.

Brittany seafood tart

Serves 6
Preparation time: 20 minutes
Cooking time: 42 minutes

1 tablespoon unsalted butter

2 baby leeks, white stems sliced

8 oz shelled fresh scallops, cleaned

2 teaspoons brandy

1 cup heavy cream

1 tablespoon tomato paste

1 garlic clove, finely chopped

2 eggs, beaten

2⅓ cups shredded Gruyère cheese

½ teaspoon cayenne

½ teaspoon paprika

3½ oz cooked shelled mussels

5 oz cod or haddock fillet, skinned, boned and cubed

1 prebaked flaky pastry shell (see page 10), in a 9 inch diameter, 1¼ inch deep tart pan

freshly ground black pepper

Preheat the oven to 350°F.

Melt the butter in a skillet, add the leeks and let them soften over gentle heat, then set aside.

In the same skillet, brown the scallops over medium to high heat for 1–2 minutes without overcooking them. Reduce the heat to medium, add the brandy, and flambé (see tip below), then remove the scallops from the heat and set aside.

Put the cream into a large bowl and add the tomato paste, garlic, eggs, cheese, and spices. Season with only black pepper because Gruyère cheese is already salty.

Place all the seafood, including the raw fish, in the cooked pastry shell. Add the leeks. Cover with the egg mixture and bake in the oven for 35–40 minutes, or until nice and golden.

Serve warm from the oven, with a fresh herb salad of dill and spinach with a tangy lemon and olive oil dressing.

Tip

To flambé (meaning "flamed" in French) first make sure your pan is over low to medium heat, add your alcohol to the pan at arms reach, then light the lip of the pan with a long match or taper. Stand well back as the flames ignite and wait for a few seconds for the alcohol to burn off.

I really like the fact that thanks to local farmers' markets you can now easily buy so many varieties of vegetables and fruits. I love heirloom tomatoes. They make great colorful salads, and are so flavorsome, too. This is a savory version of the classic tarte Tatin.

Upside-down heirloom tomato tatin

Serves 8

Preparation time: 15 minutes

Cooking time: 50 minutes

1 lb store-bought puff pastry or ½ quantity homemade puff pastry (see pages 16–17)

all-purpose flour, for dusting

2 teaspoons extra virgin olive oil

bunch of thyme, leaves picked

12 mixed heirloom tomatoes, halved

¾ cup grated Gruyère cheese

2 tablespoons whole-grain mustard

bunch of basil

salt and freshly ground black pepper

Take a 10 inch diameter, 1½ inch deep ovenproof tart dish, (or a tarte tatin pan, if you have one). Roll out the pastry dough on a lightly floured surface to about ¼ inch thick. Cut out a large circle 3 inches bigger in diameter than the dish.

Rub the inside of the dish with the olive oil. Scatter the thyme leaves over the bottom of the dish.

Season the tomatoes with salt and pepper, then place them in the dish cut side up (they must be packed tightly together because they will shrink). Bake in a preheated oven, at 400°F, for 25 minutes, then carefully pour off all the juices that have been released during cooking. Sprinkle the cheese over the top.

Using a spatula, spread the mustard carefully over the pastry circle. Place the pastry, mustard side down, on top of the tomatoes and tuck in the overhanging edges to create a crust. Prick the pastry with a knife a few times to help release the steam.

Place back in the oven and bake for 25–30 minutes, or until the pastry is golden and crisp. Place a large plate over the pie dish, hold them together firmly, then turn them over so that the tart is on the plate, being careful not to burn yourself on any hot juices. Just before serving, sprinkle basil leaves over the top of the tart.

This is delicious served warm, alongside a cold salad of mixed green beans and fava beans with a sweet shallot dressing.

1

Roll out the pastry dough and cut out a circle 3 inches bigger in diameter than your dish.

Upside-down heirloom tomato tatin

2

Oil the dish, add thyme leaves, season the tomatoes, and arrange them in the dish cut side up.

5

Divide the cheese evenly over the top.

6

Spread mustard over the pastry and drape over the tomatoes.

7

Tuck in the pastry edges, then bake in the oven.

3

Bake in the oven, then pour off any juices released from cooking.

4

Sprinkle grated cheese over the tomatoes.

8

Press a large plate over the top of the cooked tart.

9

Turn the tart upside-down onto the plate to serve.

It's funny how you try a new recipe and suddenly you just can't stop making it—I think during the week in which I came up with this combination I made it five times! It is my dream light lunch or appetizer—all the ingredients are well balanced and work so well together.

Fig, lardon, and dolcelatte tart

Serves 8

Preparation time: 20 minutes, plus chilling

Cooking time: 1 hour

For the pastry dough

2 cups all-purpose flour, plus extra for dusting

pinch of salt

2/3 cup finely chopped walnuts

1¼ sticks chilled unsalted butter, cut into pieces, plus extra for greasing

1 egg yolk

1–2 tablespoons chilled water

For the filling

8 ripe figs, cut into quarters

2 teaspoon olive oil

3½ oz lardons or bacon pieces

2/3 cup mascarpone cheese

2 eggs, beaten

¼ cup milk

2 teaspoons chopped fresh thyme, plus extra sprigs for garnish

1⅓ cups crumbled dolcelatte cheese or gorgonzola cheese

salt and freshly ground black pepper

Lightly grease a 9½ x 3 inch, 1¼ inch deep tart pan, or a pan of similar dimensions.

To make the pastry dough, place the flour, salt, and chopped walnuts in a bowl and rub in the chilled butter until the mixture resembles fine bread crumbs. Stir in the egg yolk, then gradually add enough of the chilled water until the mixture comes together to form a firm dough—add the water a little at a time to prevent the mixture from becoming too sticky.

Roll the dough out on a floured surface and line the pan (see page 18). Chill in the refrigerator for 30 minutes.

Meanwhile, preheat the oven to 400°F.

Once chilled, prick the pastry all over with a fork, cover with a sheet of wax paper, and fill the pan with pie weights or dried beans. Bake for 20 minutes, then remove the paper and weights and bake for another 10 minutes, or until the pastry begins to turn golden.

Arrange the figs in circles to cover the bottom of the tart pan. Put into the oven and cook for 10–12 minutes, or until they begin to soften. Heat the oil in a skillet and lightly sauté the lardons until they just begin to brown. Remove from the heat and set aside.

Place the mascarpone in a medium bowl and stir to soften, then add the beaten eggs and milk and stir until you have a smooth mixture. Season with a little salt and pepper and add the chopped thyme.

Sprinkle the cooked lardons and the crumbled dolcelatte over the top of the softened figs, then pour over the mascarpone and egg mixture. Finally, sprinkle over some small sprigs of thyme and bake in the oven for 20–25 minutes, or until the filling is set and golden.

I like this tart served at room temperature, with some lightly dressed salad greens.

This is a recipe from eastern France. I think it is probably the most popular savory tart in the world, but so often it is done badly. It's a really simple recipe—it doesn't require many ingredients, and it's so good eaten hot from the oven.

"Real" quiche Lorraine

Serves 8

Preparation time: 15 minutes

Cooking time: 45 minutes

1 prebaked flaky pastry shell (see page 10), in an 8½ inch diameter, 1¾ inch deep tart pan

4 eggs

2 tablespoons butter

1 teaspoon olive oil

2 shallots, finely chopped

5 oz lardons or bacon pieces

1 cup heavy cream

1 cup finely grated Gruyère cheese

½ teaspoon freshly grated nutmeg

salt and freshly ground black pepper

Preheat the oven to 400°F.

Brush the inside of the cooked pastry shell with one of the eggs, lightly beaten. Bake in the oven for 8–10 minutes, or until golden (this is to seal the tart). Let cool. Reduce the oven temperature to 350°C.

Heat the butter and olive oil in a skillet over low heat. Add the shallots and cook gently until golden, stirring occasionally. Remove from the skillet and set aside.

Add the lardons to the same skillet with any juices left behind from the shallots, and sauté until golden. Remove the lardons from the skillet, add to the shallots, and let cool.

Beat the remaining eggs in a bowl and stir in the cream, cheese, and nutmeg, and season with salt and pepper. Remember that the lardons and cheese are already naturally salty.

Sprinkle the cooked lardons and shallots across the bottom of the pastry shell and transfer the cream mixture to a large measuring cup. Place the tart pan on the oven shelf, then pour the cream filling over the lardons, filling the shell right to the top.

Bake in the oven for 25–30 minutes, or until the filling has set and the top of the quiche is wonderful and golden.

Serve warm accompanied by a leafy salad with a walnut oil dressing.

Tip

Always buy whole nutmeg and use it freshly grated. It will have far more flavor than the ground nutmeg available in jars.

The region of Brittany where I come from grows a lot of the vegetables and salad found in France, and Belgian endive, a type of chicory, is a popular salad green. This tart is inspired by a childhood recipe for baked endive with honey-roast ham. I've made it as a tart and replaced the roast ham with prosciutto.

Belgian endive and prosciutto tart

Serves 8

Preparation time: 15 minutes

Cooking time: 45 minutes

4 heads of Belgian endive (the ones with red veining will look better)

8 slices of prosciutto

2 eggs

¾ cup plus 2 tablespoons heavy cream

2 teaspoons finely chopped fresh chives

⅓ cup freshly grated Parmesan cheese

1 prebaked whole-wheat flaky pastry shell (see page 10), in a 9 inch diameter, 1¾ inch deep tart pan

salt and freshly ground black pepper

Steam the Belgian endives for 12 minutes, or until a knife goes in easily. Place on paper towels to drain and cool.

Preheat the oven to 350°F.

Cut the endives in half lengthwise and wrap a slice of prosciutto around each half, leaving the tips free.

Beat the eggs in a bowl and stir in the cream, chives, Parmesan, salt, and pepper (remember that prosciutto is salty).

Place the wrapped endives in the cooked pastry shell, with the tips resting on the edge. Pour the cream mixture over the endives to fill the tart.

Bake in the oven for 25–30 minutes, or until set and golden. Be careful not to overcook the tart or the prosciutto will dry out.

Tip

Drain the endives thoroughly before wrapping them in the prosciutto.

These individual tarts are my favorite appetizers for when I'm in a rush or just want a light meal.

Tomato and Dijon mustard tartes fines

Serves 6

Preparation time: 15 minutes

Cooking time: 15 minutes

1 lb store-bought puff pastry or ½ quantity homemade puff pastry (see page 16)

all-purpose flour, for dusting

1 egg yolk, beaten

6 teaspoons Dijon mustard

6 plum tomatoes, sliced lengthwise

fresh or dried oregano, for sprinkling

olive oil

6 (4 oz) buffalo mozzarella balls, drained

bunch of wild arugula

salt and freshly ground black pepper

Preheat the oven to 400°F.

Roll out the pastry on a lightly floured surface to ⅓ inch thick. Using a pastry cutter or a saucer as a template, cut out six 6 inch circles and place them on 2 baking sheets.

Brush the egg yolk around the inside edges of the circles with a pastry brush. Lightly prick the centers with a fork. Spread a good layer of mustard in the center of each circle, keeping the glazed edge clean.

Place the tomatoes overlapping on top of the mustard. Season with salt and pepper and sprinkle with either fresh or dried oregano and a light drizzle of olive oil.

Bake in the oven for 15–20 minutes, or until the pastry is nice and golden.

Place the warm tarts on individual serving plates. Using a sharp knife, cut a deep cross in the top of each mozzarella ball. Place a ball in the center of each tart and stuff with fresh arugula. Drizzle with olive oil and serve.

Tip

You can replace the mustard with a tomato or basil pesto.

This colorful tart is great as an appetizer or as a main dish served with some crunchy stir-fried greens, such as baby bok choy.

Mushroom, feta, and cherry tomato tart

Serves 6

Preparation time: 10 minutes

Cooking time: 45 minutes

1 cup halved cherry tomatoes (mixed colors)

2 tablespoons olive oil

1 garlic clove, finely chopped

10 oz mixed portobello mushrooms

4 eggs

1 cup crumbled feta cheese

2 tablespoons snipped chives

1 prebaked flaky pastry shell (see page 10), in a 9 inch diameter, 1¼ inch deep tart pan

salt and freshly ground black pepper

Cut the tomatoes in half and place them in a roasting pan. Bake in a preheated oven, at 350°F, for 10 minutes, or until the tomatoes start to soften slightly. Set aside and leave the oven on.

Heat the olive oil in a skillet. Add the garlic and mushrooms and sauté over gentle heat for 10 minutes, turning them occasionally. Pat the mushrooms dry with paper towels, if necessary, and set aside.

Beat the eggs in a bowl, add the feta cheese, and mix well. Stir in the mushrooms and chives, then season with salt and pepper.

Pour the mushroom mixture into the cooked pastry shell and arrange the roasted tomatoes on top. Bake in the oven for 25–30 minutes, or until golden.

Tip

Never wash mushrooms—simply wipe them clean with a sheet of paper towel.

Just seeing the beautiful colors of this tart will give you an appetite … and it makes such a nice fresh appetizer, served either hot or cold.

Zucchini ribbon and roasted pepper tart

Serves 8

Preparation time: 15 minutes

Cooking time: 50 minutes

1 large red bell pepper

1 large yellow bell pepper

2 tablespoons olive oil

1 large zucchini, thinly sliced lengthwise

2 eggs

1¼ cups heavy cream

½ cup grated red Leicester or cheddar cheese

a few sprigs of fresh rosemary, tender leaves picked

1 prebaked flaky pastry shell with dried herbes de Provence added (see page 10), in an 8½ inch square, 1¼ inch deep tart pan

salt and freshly ground black pepper

Using kebab skewers or a fork, hold the bell peppers over a gas flame until the skin bubbles and blackens in places. (If you don't have gas, blanch the bell peppers in boiling water for 2–3 minutes.) Put them into a bowl, cover with a clean dish towel, and let cool. Remove and discard the blackened skins, then quarter and seed the bell peppers.

Heat the olive oil in a hot skillet and gently cook the zucchini ribbons for 5 minutes, without breaking them. Remove them from the skillet and set aside. Add the bell peppers to the skillet and cook for 10 minutes or until soft, then set aside. Meanwhile, preheat the oven to 350°F.

In a bowl, mix together the eggs, cream, cheese, and rosemary leaves. Season with salt and pepper.

Arrange the zucchini and bell peppers elegantly in the cooked pastry shell and pour the cream mixture over the vegetables. Bake in the oven for 30–35 minutes, or until set and golden.

This tart is delicious hot or cold but is better eaten on the day it's made, otherwise the juices from the bell peppers will make the lovely Provençal crust soggy.

Brittany, the region of France that I come from, is the biggest producer of artichokes, and trust me—I've eaten my fair share of them! But it was only when I started to travel to Italy that I discovered a new way of eating them. This tart is about all the fabulous flavors of the southern part of that country.

Artichoke and black olive tart

Serves 8

Preparation time: 10 minutes

Cooking time: 25 minutes

5–6 marinated artichokes (7 oz), drained and cut into quarters

1 cup coarsely chopped, pitted ripe black Kalamata olives

1 prebaked flaky pastry shell with ¼ cup grated Parmesan cheese added (see page 10), in a 9 inch diameter, 1¼ inch deep tart pan

5 oz soft goat cheese

scant ½ cup heavy cream

3 eggs

1 tablespoon fresh thyme leaves

salt and freshly ground black pepper

Preheat the oven to 350°F.

Arrange the artichokes and olives in the bottom of the cooked pastry shell.

Blend the goat cheese with the cream, eggs, and thyme, then season with salt and pepper.

Pour the mixture over the artichokes and olives and bake in the oven for 25 minutes, or until just set and light golden.

Tip

Buy whole olives and remove the pits before using—they will have more flavor than those you can buy already pitted.

This is my twist on a very traditional salad. I made it as a tart because, to be honest, these ingredients are so good together, whether raw or baked.

Waldorf-inspired tart

Serves 8

Preparation time: 20 minutes

Cooking time: 50 minutes

7 oz Roquefort, or other blue cheese

¾ cup plus 2 tablespoons crème fraîche

4 eggs

½ teaspoon freshly grated nutmeg

2 teaspoon olive oil

2 shallots, finely chopped

4 celery sticks, cut into ½ inch chunks

1⅔ cups roasted walnut halves

⅓ cup halved red grapes

1 prebaked puff pastry crust (see pages 16–17), rolled to 10 x 8 inches, using 12 oz store-bought or ⅓ quantity homemade puff pastry

1 cup grated French Comté or other nutty hard cheese

freshly ground black pepper

Preheat the oven to 350°C.

Using your fingers, crumble the blue cheese into a bowl. Mix in the crème fraîche, then beat in the eggs, nutmeg, and pepper.

Heat the olive oil in a skillet. Add the shallots and sauté over medium heat until golden, then remove them from the skillet and set aside. Add the celery to the skillet and gently sauté for 10 minutes—it should still be slightly crunchy. Just before removing the skillet from the heat, toss in the walnuts, grapes, and sautéed shallots. Mix well, then spoon into the cooked puff pastry crust.

Pour the blue cheese mixture over the tart, then sprinkle with the Comté cheese and bake in the oven for 35 minutes, or until set and golden.

Tip

Roquefort has no rind, but if you use another blue cheese you may need to remove the rind before using it in the tart.

When I was growing up we always had fantastic food at home. One of our treats was blood sausage served with baked apples. It's a great combination … this is my take on one of my favorite childhood recipes.

Blood sausage and apple tart

Serves 8

Preparation time: 15 minutes

Cooking time: 40 minutes

4 tablespoons unsalted butter

2 Pippin or Granny Smith apples, peeled, cored, and quartered

⅔ cup heavy cream

½ cup milk

2 extra-large eggs

2 teaspoon ground allspice

8 oz blood sausage

1 prebaked flaky pastry shell (see page 10), in a 9 inch diameter, 1¼ inch deep tart pan

2 tablespoons thyme leaves

2 bay leaves

salt and freshly ground black pepper

Preheat the oven to 350°F.

Melt the butter in a large skillet. Add the apple quarters and sauté over medium heat until they have a nice golden color but are not mushy. Remove the apples from the skillet and set aside.

In a bowl, mix the cream with the milk, eggs, and allspice, and season with salt and pepper. Cut the blood sausage into chunky pieces and place in the cooked pastry shell. Tuck the apple quarters in between the pieces of blood sausage.

Sprinkle with the thyme leaves. Break up the bay leaves and arrange on top. Pour in the egg and cream mixture and bake in the oven for 30 minutes, or until set and golden. Carefully remove and discard the bay leaves.

A warm salad of root vegetables is the perfect companion for this unusual but delicious tart.

Tip

Firm apples are best for this, because they will not break up in the skillet while you sauté them.

I just love the way the recent trend of the farmers' market has made us all rediscover our vegetables and fruits. I really like the mixed-color heritage beets, and this tart is just a little ray of sunshine. The broccoli is perfect for cutting through the earthiness of the beautiful roasted beets.

Heritage beet and broccoli tart

Serves 8

Preparation time: 20 minutes

Cooking time: 1 hour 5 minutes

grated zest and juice of 1/2 an orange

1 tablespoon olive oil

1 teaspoon light brown sugar

5–6 raw heritage beets (1 lb), peeled and quartered

1 2/3 cups coarsely chopped broccoli

1 prebaked flaky pastry shell (see page 10), in a 9 inch diameter, 1 1/4 inch deep tart pan

2/3 cup mascarpone cheese

1/4 cup heavy cream

2 eggs, beaten

1/2 teaspoon freshly grated nutmeg

salt and freshly ground black pepper

snipped fresh chives, to garnish

Put the orange zest and juice into a bowl with the olive oil and sugar and mix together. Place the beet quarters in a roasting pan, pour the orange mixture over them, and toss to coat. Roast in a preheated oven, at 400°F, for 35–40 minutes, or until tender. If necessary, cover with aluminum foil halfway through cooking to prevent them from overbrowning.

Bring a large saucepan of lightly salted water to a boil. Have ready a bowl of cold water. Add the broccoli to the boiling water and cook for 2 minutes. Drain, then plunge the broccoli into the cold water. When cold, drain well and place in the cooked pastry shell. Arrange the beets on top.

Reduce the oven heat to 350°F. Put the mascarpone and cream into a bowl and mix until smooth. Stir in the eggs and nutmeg, then season with salt and pepper. Pour the mixture over the beets and bake in the oven for 25 minutes, or until just set and light golden.

Sprinkle with chives just before serving and serve with onion marmalade (see page 95).

Tip

Heritage beets are often available in farmers' markets—dark red, golden, even striped!

Some of the classic combinations are still the best, and it would be silly to try to update them. Rich smoked salmon, an abundance of fresh dill, and spicy French grain mustard ... a perfect appetizer or light meal.

Salmon, whole-grain mustard, and dill tartlets

Serves 6
Preparation time: 10 minutes
Cooking time: 25 minutes

1 tablespoon butter

4 scallions, finely chopped

6 oz smoked salmon, cut into strips

6 prebaked flaky pastry shells (see page 10), each in individual 4 inch diameter tart pans

2 eggs, beaten

⅔ cup crème fraîche

1 tablespoon chopped fresh dill

2 teaspoon whole-grain mustard

salt and freshly ground black pepper

Preheat the oven to 350°F.

Melt the butter in a small skillet and gently sauté the scallions for 2–3 minutes, or until softened. Remove from the skillet and let cool.

Arrange the smoked salmon in the bottom of the cooked pastry shells.

In a bowl, mix together the eggs, crème fraîche, dill, mustard, and cooled scallions and season with salt and pepper. Pour the mixture into the tart shells, pulling up some of the salmon through the egg mixture so it is visible on the surface.

Bake in the oven for 18–20 minutes, or until just set and golden.

This very summery tart is perfect for an alfresco lunch or picnic. The goat cheese cuts through the sweetness of the red onion marmalade and roasted peppers, and a salad of arugula, fresh basil, and roasted pine nuts will make it even more delicious!

Roasted red pepper and goat cheese tart

Serves 6

Preparation time: 15 minutes

Cooking time: 55 minutes

3 red bell peppers

1 garlic clove, crushed

2 tablespoons olive oil

1 red onion, thinly sliced

2 tablespoons balsamic vinegar

1 prebaked flaky pastry shell (see page 10), in a 9 inch diameter, 1¼ inch deep tart pan

7 oz goat cheese (Sainte Maure, if possible), sliced

2 teaspoons chopped fresh thyme, plus extra to garnish

3 eggs, beaten

⅔ cup plain Greek yogurt

salt and freshly ground black pepper

Cut the bell peppers into quarters and remove the seeds. Place the bell peppers on a roasting pan with the garlic and drizzle 1 tablespoon of the oil over them. Roast in a preheated oven, at 350°F, for about 20 minutes or until the peppers are nice and soft. Set aside and leave the oven on.

Put the remaining oil into a saucepan over low heat and add the onion. Cook for 5 minutes, or until the onion begins to soften, then add the balsamic vinegar. Cook for another 5 minutes, until all the vinegar has reduced and you are left with a red onion marmalade. Spread this evenly over the bottom of the cooked pastry shell. Arrange the roasted peppers on top, followed by the goat cheese. Sprinkle with the thyme.

Mix together the eggs and yogurt in a small bowl and season well with salt and pepper. Place the tart on a baking sheet, then pour the egg mixture over the tart.

Bake in the oven for 25–30 minutes, or until the tart is set and golden. Sprinkle thyme over the tart to garnish.

Tip

To save time, you can buy good-quality, roasted peppers that are available in jars.

This is a very flavorsome tart and you can make it as spicy as you want, but I like mine mild. A salad of greens and plenty of fresh cilantro is the perfect accompaniment.

Curried chicken tart

Serves 8

Preparation time: 15 minutes

Cooking time: 50 minutes

12 oz store-bought puff pastry or ⅓ quantity homemade puff pastry (see pages 16–17)

all-purpose flour, for dusting

2 tablespoons vegetable oil

1 onion, thinly sliced

13 oz boneless, skinless chicken breasts, cut into strips

¼ cup Thai red curry paste

1⅔ cups coconut milk

1 tomato, peeled, seeded, and chopped

1¼ cups chopped canned or fresh pineapple

2 eggs

bunch of fresh cilantro, coarsely chopped

salt and freshly ground black pepper

Preheat the oven to 350°F.

Roll out the pastry on a lightly floured surface to ¼ inch thick and use it to line a 9 inch diameter, 1¾ inch deep tart pan, then prebake (see page 19).

Heat the oil in a large skillet, then add the onion and sauté gently until it has browned and softened. Add the chicken and stir-fry for 2–3 minutes. Stir in the curry paste, half the coconut milk, the tomato, and the chopped pineapple. Simmer for 10–12 minutes, stirring occasionally, until the sauce has greatly reduced and thickened. Let cool for 5 minutes.

Blend the eggs in a bowl with the rest of the coconut milk and add the cilantro. Stir into the curry mixture, then season with salt and pepper.

Fill the cooked pastry shell with the mixture and bake in the oven for 30 minutes, or until set and golden.

Serve warm, alongside a fresh cilantro salad dressed with sesame oil and finely chopped shallots.

I grew up eating vol-au-vents with the traditional chicken and sweetbread filling. My mom was very selective about where she bought them—the best ones contained a lot of sweetbreads, which are so succulent when prepared well. This is my take on that 1970s classic, made into a pie.

Chicken and sweetbread pie

Serves 10

Preparation time: 25 minutes, plus soaking

Cooking time: 1 hour 5 minutes

8 oz sweetbreads

3¼ lb chicken pieces

⅔ cup all-purpose flour

2 tablespoons olive oil

6 tablespoons butter

16 shallots, peeled

3½ cups halved button mushrooms

1 garlic clove, crushed

1¼ cups dry white wine

scant 1 cup chicken stock

2 tablespoons brandy

¼ teaspoon ground nutmeg

2 tablespoons chopped fresh parsley

2 bay leaves

12 oz store-bought puff pastry or ⅓ quantity homemade puff pastry (see pages 16–17)

all-purpose flour, for dusting

1 egg, beaten

salt and freshly ground black pepper

Put the sweetbreads into a bowl and cover with cold water. Cover the bowl and refrigerate for 3 hours, or overnight.

When you are ready to make the pie, preheat the oven to 350°F.

Bring a saucepan of water to a boil. Drain the sweetbreads and add to the pan. Boil for 1 minute, then drain. Remove the membrane from the sweetbreads, then cut them into 1 inch pieces.

Roll the chicken pieces in ⅓ cup of the flour to lightly coat. Heat the oil and 2 tablespoons of the butter in a large skillet, and cook the chicken, in batches, until browned all over. Transfer the chicken to a large ovenproof dish, about 12 x 8 x 2 inches. Add the shallots, mushrooms, and garlic to the skillet and cook, stirring, for 3 minutes. Transfer the mixture to the ovenproof dish.

Add the rest of the butter to the skillet and let it melt. Add the remaining flour and cook, stirring, until the mixture is bubbling. Remove the skillet from the heat, then gradually stir in the wine, stock, brandy, nutmeg, and parsley. Season with salt and pepper. Bring to a boil, stirring, and simmer until thickened.

Pour the sauce over the chicken and add the bay leaves and sweetbreads. Roll out the pastry on a lightly floured surface to a size a little larger than your dish. Brush the rim of the dish with some of the beaten egg, cover the pie with the pastry, and trim off any excess. Press the pastry edges against the rim of the dish to seal and crimp the edges (see tip below). Brush the pastry all over with more beaten egg.

Bake in the oven for 50 minutes, or until the pastry is crisp and golden.

Tip

To crimp the edges of a pie, press your index and middle fingers onto the pie edge, then use your index finger on your other hand to push the dough between your two fingers to create a scalloped edge. Repeat all the way around the pie.

I love cooking with chorizo—it brings so much flavor, heat, and color to a dish. However, make sure you use the chorizo that's meant for cooking. The trick is to release all the delicious oils from the chorizo to get the very best flavor from it.
My friend Amanda's recipe inspired me to make this pie.

Iberian chicken pie

Serves 6

Preparation time: 10 minutes

Cooking time: 45 minutes

1 tablespoon butter

1 tablespoon olive oil

1 lb chicken, cut into cubes

7 oz chorizo, sliced

2 garlic cloves, finely chopped

1 teaspoon cayenne pepper

1 (14½ oz) can of diced tomatoes

2 teaspoons paprika

1 tablespoon chopped fresh flat-leaf parsley

1 quantity (14½ oz) flaky pastry dough (see page 10)

all-purpose flour, for dusting

1 egg, beaten

salt and freshly ground black pepper

Heat the butter and oil in a skillet and sauté the chicken over medium heat until it starts to brown. Remove from the skillet and set aside. Add the chorizo to the skillet and sauté for a few minutes until it starts to release its oil, then add the garlic and cayenne and cook for a minute or so, stirring to make sure they don't burn.

Add the tomatoes and paprika and return the chicken to the skillet. Bring to a boil, then reduce the heat and let the sauce simmer for 10 minutes.

Meanwhile, preheat the oven to 350°F.

Season the sauce with salt and pepper and stir in the parsley. Spoon the mixture into a large 3¼ quart ovenproof dish, about 12 x 8 x 2 inches.

Roll out the dough on a lightly floured surface. Brush the rim of the ovenproof dish with some of the beaten egg. Cover the pie with the pastry and trim off any excess. Use the trimmings to make leaf shapes to decorate the top of the pastry, if desired, using the beaten egg to hold them in place. Press the pastry edges against the rim of the dish to seal. Brush the pastry all over with more beaten egg.

Bake in the oven for 25–30 minutes, or until the top of the pie is crisp and golden.

These cute little casseroles make a perfect appetizer for a dinner party or lunch—the crunchy topping is a great contrast to the creamy filling.

Scallop and zucchini crumb pie

Serves 6

Preparation time: 20 minutes

Cooking time: 45 minutes

6 tablespoons unsalted butter

1 onion, finely chopped

4 carrots, finely diced

3 leeks (only the white part), sliced thinly

1 tablespoon chopped tarragon

½ tablespoon chopped dill

2½ cups diced zucchini

scant 1 cup fish stock

2 tablespoons flour

1 tablespoon of dry white wine

2 tablespoons heavy cream

12 fresh, shelled scallops, cleaned, defrosted if frozen

30 fresh, peeled jumbo shrimp

salt and freshly ground black pepper

For the crumb topping

5 tablespoons unsalted butter, chopped into pieces

1⅓ cups whole-wheat flour

2 teaspoons dried mixed herbs

½ cup finely grated Parmesan cheese

Heat the butter in a skillet and gently sauté the onion until soft. Add the carrots and leeks, cover, and cook over low heat for 10 minutes, stirring occasionally.

Meanwhile, preheat the oven to 350°F.

Add the tarragon, dill, and zucchini to the skillet and stir, cover, and cook for another 5 minutes. Season with salt and pepper.

In a small saucepan, heat up the fish stock. Whisk in the flour a little at a time, then simmer for 1 minute. In a small bowl, mix together the wine and cream, add to the hot stock, then season.

Place 2 scallops and 5 shrimp in each of 6 individual casserole dishes. Spoon the vegetable mixture on top and pour the liquid mixture over it.

To make the crumb topping, rub all the ingredients together with the tips of your fingers until you get a chunky type of bread crumbs. Cover each casserole with a good layer of the crumbs.

Bake in the oven for 25–30 minutes, or until the topping is nice and golden and the sauce is bubbling. Serve immediately, with soda bread to soak up all the delicious juices.

I just love seafood. I don't cook it often enough, but, when I do, this simple pie is my favorite. It's a meal on its own, with the rich sauce and all the yummy, chunky seafood. I hope your guests will love it as much as mine do.

Seafood and potato pie

Serves 6

Preparation time: 35 minutes

Cooking time: 1 hour 5 minutes

2 cups milk

2 bay leaves

6 oz shelled scallops, cleaned

11 oz smoked haddock

5 red-skinned or white round potatoes (1¼ lb), peeled and cut into ¼ inch thick slices

1 stick butter

2 celery sticks, thinly sliced

3 tablespoons all-purpose flour

2 tablespoons crème fraîche

1 tablespoon chopped dill

7 oz cooked, peeled jumbo shrimp

3 oz cooked, shelled mussels

salt and freshly ground black pepper

Preheat the oven to 400°F.

Pour the milk into a large saucepan, add the bay leaves, season with black pepper, and bring to a boil. Add the scallops and cook for only 1 minute. Remove them with a slotted spoon and set aside. Add the smoked haddock to the milk, cover, and simmer for 3 minutes. Remove from the heat and let rest in the hot milk for 5 minutes.

Remove the fish from the milk and strain the milk into a small bowl, discarding the bay leaves. Break the fish into large flakes, discarding any skin or bones, and set aside.

Cook the potato slices in a large saucepan of lightly salted water for 5–6 minutes, or until just tender. Drain well.

Melt 6 tablespoons of the butter in a clean saucepan and gently sauté the celery for 10 minutes, stirring occasionally, until softened but not browned. Stir in the flour and cook for 2 minutes. Remove from the heat and gradually blend in the milk, stirring continuously. Return to the heat and slowly bring to a boil, still stirring continuously. Simmer for 2 minutes, or until thickened.

Remove from the heat, stir in the crème fraîche and dill, then season with salt and pepper. Gently stir in the scallops, smoked haddock, shrimp, and mussels.

Spoon into a 2 quart ovenproof dish, about 10½ x 8 x 1¾ inches. Arrange the potatoes on top, overlapping them in layers to cover. Melt the remaining butter and brush over the potatoes.

Bake in the oven for 40–45 minutes, or until golden and bubbling.

These cute little pies (see previous page) are full of North African flavor. The spices and chickpeas are fabulous, but the best bit for me is the aroma while the pies are baking, when the puff pastry starts to cook with the freshly crushed cumin seeds ... Delish!

Lamb and Moroccan spice pies

Serves 4

Preparation time: 15 minutes

Cooking time: 50 minutes

1 tablespoon olive oil

1 red onion, finely chopped

1 garlic clove, crushed

2 teaspoons paprika

2 teaspoons ground cumin

1 teaspoon ground cinnamon

1 lb ground lamb

1 (14½ oz) can of diced tomatoes

1 tablespoon tomato paste

1 (15 oz) can of chickpeas (garbanzo beans), drained and rinsed

⅓ cup raisins

15 dried apricots, chopped

2 tablespoons fresh chopped mint

12 oz store-bought puff pastry or ⅓ quantity homemade puff pastry (see pages 16–17)

all-purpose flour, for dusting

1 egg, beaten

½ teaspoons cumin seeds, lightly crushed

salt and freshly ground black pepper

Heat the oil in a large saucepan. Add the onion and garlic and sauté gently over low heat for 5 minutes, until softened. Add the ground spices and sauté for 1 minute. Increase the heat slightly, add the lamb, and stir-fry until browned.

Stir in the diced tomatoes, tomato paste, chickpeas, raisins, apricots, and mint. Cover and simmer for 20 minutes, stirring occasionally.

Meanwhile, preheat the oven to 400°F.

Season the mixture with salt and pepper, then divide among 4 individual 1 cup ovenproof dishes and let cool.

Roll out the pastry on a lightly floured surface and cut out 4 circles slightly bigger than the diameter of the top of the dishes. Brush the rims of the dishes with some of the beaten egg, cover each pie with a pastry lid, and trim off any excess. Press the pastry edges against the rim of the dishes to seal and crimp the edges (see tip on page 57). With a sharp knife, make several slashes across the center of each pastry, but do not pierce all the way through. Brush each pastry all over with beaten egg and sprinkle with the cumin seeds.

Place the dishes on baking sheets and bake in the oven for 20 minutes, or until puffed up and golden.

Tip

Frying ground spices for a minute or so helps to bring out the flavors.

These autumnal individual pies make a perfect vegetarian dish. Both the mushroom and the squash add a lovely earthy flavor and texture ... I often use this recipe as a side dish to accompany a traditional roast and my guests love the novelty of it.

Butternut squash and mushroom pies

Serves 4

Preparation time: 20 minutes

Cooking time: 50 minutes

1 tablespoon butter

1 large leek, split lengthwise and sliced

1 garlic clove, finely chopped

8 oz cremini mushrooms, quartered

1 small butternut squash (about 1 lb), peeled and cut into small chunks

1 cup vegetable stock

¼ cup crème fraîche

1 tablespoon chopped fresh chives

12 oz store-bought puff pastry or ⅓ quantity homemade puff pastry (see pages 16–17)

all-purpose flour, for dusting

1 egg, beaten

salt and freshly ground black pepper

Preheat the oven to 350°F.

Melt the butter in a skillet over low heat and gently sauté the leek and garlic for about 7 minutes, or until softened. Add the mushrooms and cook for 4–5 minutes. Add the squash and cook for another minute, then pour in the stock, cover, and simmer for 5 minutes.

Stir the crème fraîche and chives into the vegetables, then check the seasoning and divide among 4 individual 1 cup pie dishes.

Divide the puff pastry into 4 equal pieces and roll each one out on a lightly floured surface to fit the dishes. Brush the rims of the dishes with some of the beaten egg, cover each pie with a pastry lid, and trim off any excess. Press the pastry edges against the rim of the dish to seal and crimp the edges (see tip on page 57).

Brush the pastry all over with beaten egg and bake in the oven for 25–30 minutes, or until golden and crisp.

How much more wintry and festive could this recipe sound? It's a true old-fashioned pie and I sometimes decorate the top so that it becomes a gorgeous centerpiece.

Turkey and chestnut pie

Serves 6–8

Preparation time: 20 minutes

Cooking time: 55 minutes

2 tablespoons unsalted butter

1 onion, finely chopped

1⅓ cups finely diced carrots

2¼ cups thinly sliced leeks

1 cup heavy cream

⅔ cup chicken stock

1 tablespoon finely chopped tarragon

5 cups small, cooked turkey pieces

1 (7 oz) jar cooked, peeled chestnuts, drained

12 oz store-bought puff pastry or ⅓ quantity homemade puff pastry (see pages 16–17)

all-purpose flour, for dusting

1 egg, beaten

salt and freshly ground black pepper

Melt the butter in a large skillet and gently sauté the onion over medium heat until soft. Add the carrots and leeks and cook for another 5 minutes.

Add the cream, stock, and tarragon. Simmer for 10–12 minutes, or until the sauce starts to thicken.

Meanwhile, preheat the oven to 350°F.

Season with salt and pepper, then add the turkey and the chestnuts to the skillet, being careful not to break them up when stirring. Simmer for another 5 minutes.

Spoon the filling into a 9½ x 7 inch shallow ovenproof dish. Roll out the pastry to a ¼ inch thickness on a lightly floured surface. Brush the rim of the dish with some of the beaten egg, cover the pie with the pastry, and trim off any excess. Press the pastry edges against the rim of the dish to seal. Brush the pastry all over with beaten egg and make a couple of little holes in the middle of the pastry with the point of a sharp knife to let the steam escape.

Bake in the oven for 30–35 minutes, or until the pastry is all puffed up and golden and some of the juices are escaping.

This pie is great served with some exotic wild rice on the side.

Tip

Chestnuts can be bought in jars or pouches, already cooked and peeled, from specialty stores and online, which saves a lot of preparation time.

This is another Spanish inspiration using spicy and colorful chorizo, but this time I am using fresh jumbo shrimp and Spanish rice as a filling for a pie. It is truly a complete meal in one dish, and the combination of the rice and the golden pastry works very well with the lovely spicy juices.

Shrimp and chorizo pie

Serves 6

Preparation time: 10 minutes

Cooking time: 45 minutes

1 quantity (14½ oz) flaky pastry dough (see page 10)

all-purpose flour, for dusting

butter, for greasing

7 oz chorizo, thickly sliced

1 lb jumbo shrimp, shelled and deveined

2 garlic cloves, crushed

2 teaspoons chopped parsley

1 tablespoon finely chopped basil

⅔ cup tomato puree or tomato sauce

2 cups cooked Spanish rice or risotto rice

1 teaspoon paprika

pinch of saffron

⅔ cup fresh peas

1 teaspoon salt

1 teaspoon freshly ground black pepper

1 egg, beaten

Preheat the oven to 400°F. Grease a 10½ x 8 x 1¾ inch ovenproof dish.

Roll out two-thirds of the dough on a lightly floured surface and use it to line the dish (see page 18). Roll out the remaining dough to make the pie lid and set aside.

Put all the ingredients, except for the egg, into a bowl and stir to combine. Turn the mixture into the ovenproof dish.

Moisten the edge of the pastry with half the beaten egg. Drape the pastry lid on top and crimp to seal (see tip on page 57).

Brush the pastry all over with the beaten egg to glaze, then bake in the oven for 45 minutes, or until golden. Serve hot.

I am a great fan of seafood pie, but I often find there is a bit too much going on with all the different ingredients. In this recipe, I've kept it simple ... nice flaky haddock and large scallops, cooked in a creamy mushroom sauce with plenty of fresh parsley, topped with rich buttery mashed potato.

Scallop and mushroom pie

Serves 6

Preparation time: 20 minutes

Cooking time: 40 minutes

6 russet or Yukon gold potatoes (1 lb 6 oz), peeled and cut into chunks

4 shelled scallops, cleaned, defrosted if frozen

14½ oz haddock fillets, cut into chunks

1 bay leaf

1 small onion, finely chopped

2 cups milk

6 tablespoons unsalted butter

1¾ cups sliced button mushrooms

⅓ cup all-purpose flour

¼ cup dry sherry

2 tablespoons light cream

2 tablespoons chopped parsley

salt and freshly ground black pepper

Cook the potatoes in a saucepan of boiling salted water until tender.

Meanwhile, preheat the oven to 350°F.

Separate the red coral from the scallops, then cut the white part into fairly thick slices. Put the sliced scallops and the haddock into a medium saucepan with the bay leaf, onion, and 1¼ cups of the milk. Simmer gently for 5 minutes, then add the corals and cook for another 5 minutes, until tender.

Drain and mash the potatoes with the rest of the milk and 2 tablespoons of the butter. Drain the haddock and scallops, reserving the milk. Flake the haddock, removing any skin and bones.

Melt 3 tablespoons of the butter in a large saucepan and sauté the mushrooms for 2 minutes. Stir in the flour and cook for 1 minute. Remove from the heat and gradually stir in the reserved milk. Bring to a boil, stirring continuously, then reduce the heat and simmer for 2–3 minutes, or until thick and smooth. Stir in the sherry, cream, haddock, scallops, and parsley and mix well, then season with salt and pepper.

Pour the mixture into a 10½ x 8 x 1¾ inch ovenproof dish. Spread the mashed potatoes over the top and dot with the remaining butter.

Bake in the oven for 25–30 minutes, or until the top has browned.

I made my first game pie when I was working for Albert and Michel Roux. I had never made a savory pie before, but this is now part of my repertoire.

Game pies

Serves 6

Preparation time: 25 minutes, plus chilling

Cooking time: 40 minutes

1 lb 10 oz mixed game meat, such as pheasant and venison, ground (use a food processor or ask your butcher)

2 red onions, finely chopped

⅔ cup smooth chicken liver pâté

1 garlic clove, finely chopped

2 tablespoons port

⅓ cup plus 1 tablespoon all-purpose flour, plus extra for dusting

6 crepes (thin pancakes, see tip below)

2 eggs, beaten

2 lb store-bought puff pastry or 1 quantity homemade puff pastry (see pages 16–17)

salt and freshly ground black pepper

Put the ground meat, onions, pâté, garlic, port, and flour into a large bowl and mix together. Season well with salt and pepper, then divide the filling into 6 equal balls and refrigerate for 1 hour.

Preheat the oven to 350°F.

Wrap each ball of game mixture with a crepe (this will soak up all the juices and keep the pastry crisp) and brush all over with some of the beaten egg.

Divide the pastry into 6 even pieces and roll them out on a lightly floured surface into large circles big enough to enclose a ball. Place a game ball in the center of each piece of pastry. Brush the borders of the pastry with a little more egg (this helps seal the edges together and stops the filling from oozing out), then wrap the pastry around the ball, enclosing it like a package. Place the packages on 2 baking sheets, with the seams underneath.

Brush the pastry all over with the rest of the egg, then, using a sharp knife, score curved lines from top to bottom, making sure not to pierce the pastry. Make a small hole in the top for steam to escape, then bake in the oven for 40 minutes, or until the pastry is all puffed up and golden. Serve with fine green beans.

Tip

To make crepes, follow the recipe you normally use to make pancakes, but add extra milk; the batter should still be creamy but also runny.

I am sure you find it tricky sometimes (like I do) to come up with really exciting and delicious vegetarian recipes. This one is now my favorite recipe. It has everything, from delicious vegetables to a rich cheese sauce, and has a wonderful texture, thanks to the phyllo pastry and pine nuts. You don't have to be a vegetarian to fall in love with this fabulous pie.

Summer vegetable pie

Serves 6

Preparation time: 25 minutes

Cooking time: 1¼ hours

5 red-skinned or white round potatoes (1 lb 3 oz), peeled and cut into chunks

3 tablespoons butter, melted, plus extra for greasing

3 eggs

1½ cups shredded cheddar cheese

1 tablespoon olive oil

2 garlic cloves, crushed

1 (6 oz) package fresh spinach leaves, coarsely chopped

2 cups shredded zucchini

1 cup chopped mixed red and yellow bell peppers

4 scallions, finely chopped

⅓ cup chopped chives

½ teaspoon grated nutmeg

6 sheets of phyllo pastry

1½ tablespoons pine nuts

salt and freshly ground black pepper

Cook the potatoes in a saucepan of boiling salted water until tender. Set aside to cool slightly.

Meanwhile, preheat the oven to 350°F. Grease a 9½ inch diameter, 1¾ inch deep ovenproof dish.

Beat the eggs in a large bowl and mix in the cheese. Heat the oil in a skillet, add the garlic, and cook gently over low heat for 2 minutes. Stir in the spinach and cook until the leaves have just wilted.

Add the spinach to the egg mixture, along with the potatoes, zucchini, bell peppers, scallions, chives, and nutmeg. Season with salt and pepper.

Unroll the phyllo pastry sheets and keep those you are not using covered with a damp cloth to prevent them from drying out. Line the dish with 4 sheets of phyllo, brushing each layer with melted butter and letting the edges hang over the sides.

Spoon in the vegetable filling and spread it evenly. Fold the edges of the phyllo toward the center, brushing with more butter as you work. Brush the remaining phyllo pastry sheets all over with butter and cover the top of the pie, scrunching the pastry to fit. Brush the top of the pie with butter and sprinkle the pine nuts over it.

Bake in the oven for 35 minutes, or until crisp and golden. Serve hot.

This recipe is a great dish to serve alongside a glorious roasted chicken. It's a show-stopper, first, for its lattice top and, second, for the way all the ingredients come together while steaming away under the pastry while in the oven—all the flavors of spring in a gorgeous flaky pie.

Braised lettuce lattice pie

Serves 8

Preparation time: 15 minutes

Cooking time: 40 minutes

2 tablespoons butter

1 onion, finely sliced

3½ oz lardons or bacon pieces

1¾ cups peas, defrosted if frozen

6 baby Boston lettuce, cut in half

bunch of fresh mint, finely shredded

scant ½ cup vegetable stock

12 oz store-bought puff pastry or ⅓ quantity homemade puff pastry (see pages 16–17)

1 egg, beaten

salt and freshly ground black pepper

Preheat the oven to 350°F.

Heat a skillet over moderate heat, add the butter and onion, and sauté for 4–5 minutes, until soft. Add the lardons and cook for another 5 minutes.

Place the peas and lettuce in a 10½ x 8 x 1¾ inch ovenproof dish, and add the cooked onion mixture and the mint. Pour the stock over the onions and season with salt and pepper.

Roll out the pastry on a lightly floured surface and cut into ¾ inch strips slightly longer than the dish. Brush the edges of the dish with some of the beaten egg and arrange the strips of pastry over the top in a lattice pattern.

Brush the pastry all over with beaten egg and bake in the oven for 25–30 minutes, or until golden.

For me, growing up in Brittany, pork and cider was a classic—and what a great combination. I have reinvented this childhood favorite as a pie.

Pork and cider pie

Serves 4

Preparation time: 20 minutes

Cooking time: 55 minutes

2 teaspoons olive oil

1 lb cured ham steak, coarsely chopped

1 red onion, finely chopped

2 Granny Smith or Pippin apples, peeled, cored, and diced

2 red-skinned or white round potatoes, peeled and diced

2/3 cup dry cider

2/3 cup chicken stock

2 teaspoons whole-grain mustard

2 bay leaves

1 tablespoon finely chopped thyme

1 tablespoon butter

1 tablespoon all-purpose flour, plus extra for dusting

11½ oz store-bought puff pastry or ⅓ quantity homemade puff pastry (see pages 16–17)

1 egg, beaten

salt and freshly ground black pepper

Preheat the oven to 350°F.

Heat the olive oil in a skillet. Add the cured ham and sauté until lightly golden. Add the onion, apples, potatoes, cider, stock, mustard, bay leaves, and thyme. Simmer for 5 minutes, then season with salt and pepper.

Put the butter and flour into a small bowl and mix together to make a paste. Blend in a little of the sauce from the cured ham, then stir the mixture back into the skillet. Simmer over medium heat until the sauce has thickened and become smooth and almost glossy. Pour into a 1½ quart ovenproof dish, about 8 x 6 x 2 inches.

Roll out the pastry on a lightly floured surface to ¼ inch thick. Brush the rim of the dish with some of the beaten egg, cover the pie with the pastry, and trim off any excess. Press the pastry edges against the rim of the dish to seal and brush the top with beaten egg. Make a couple of holes in the center of the pastry to let the steam out, then bake in the oven for 35–40 minutes, or until the pastry is well risen and a rich golden color.

This is best served with freshly steamed vegetables glazed in butter with sea salt crystals and plenty of chunky rustic bread.

Tip

Making a paste of butter and flour and stirring it into a sauce or casserole is a good way to thicken it.

This is a real winter treat for a time when only comfort food will do. The earthy combination of the root vegetables, the rich garlicky Toulouse sausage, and the crunchy crumb topping will be a winner for everyone.

Toulouse sausage and root vegetable pies

Serves 6

Preparation time: 20 minutes

Cooking time: 1 hour 20 minutes

2 red onions, cut into wedges

2 parsnips, cut into 2 inch chunks

4 carrots (mixed colors, if possible), cut into chunks

3 fresh beets (mixed colors if possible), cut into wedges

2 teaspoons olive oil

2 tablespoons honey

1 tablespoon chopped thyme

6 Toulouse sausages, cut into chunks

scant 1 cup heavy cream

2/3 cup chicken stock

1 2/3 cups whole-wheat flour

3/4 cup plus 1 tablespoon all-purpose flour

1 1/4 sticks unsalted butter

1 cup shredded sharp cheddar cheese

salt and freshly ground black pepper

Place all the vegetables in a roasting pan. Pour the olive oil and honey over them, add the thyme, and toss everything together using your hands. Roast in a preheated oven, at 350°F, for 50 minutes, or until the vegetables start to soften.

Leave the oven on and transfer the roasted vegetables to a large pie plate, or divide them among 6 individual large ramekins. Add the sausages, pour the cream and stock over the sausage and vegetable filling, then season with salt and pepper.

Put the flours, butter, and cheese into a large bowl and rub together using your fingertips to make a chunky crumb mixture. Sprinkle the crumb mixture over the sausage and vegetable filling and bake in the oven for 25–30 minutes, or until the crumb topping is golden.

Serve alongside a fennel salad with a walnut dressing.

Tip

You can use any combination of winter root vegetables in this recipe such as potatoes, pumpkin, or butternut squash.

The Greek island of Mykonos is one of my favorite summer destinations. Every street corner has a little café serving delicious pies made of the finest phyllo pastry and crumbly local feta cheese. This pie brings back great memories and the anticipation of my next visit to this stylish island.

Spinach phyllo pie

Serves 6

Preparation time: 15 minutes

Cooking time: 40 minutes

5 tablespoons butter

2 onions, thinly sliced

2 garlic cloves, crushed

1 lb spinach leaves, washed and coarsely chopped

1 teaspoon freshly grated nutmeg

1⅓ cups crumbled feta cheese

¾ cup drained canned chickpeas (garbanzo beans) coarsely crushed

2 eggs, beaten

4 large sheets of phyllo pastry

salt and freshly ground black pepper

Preheat the oven to 400°F.

Heat 2 tablespoons of the butter in a large skillet. Add the onions and cook until soft and turning golden, then add the garlic and cook for a couple of minutes. Add the spinach, in batches, and cook until just wilted. Cool, then spoon into a bowl (leaving behind any excess liquid from the spinach). Mix in the nutmeg, feta, chickpeas, and eggs and season with salt and pepper.

Melt the remaining butter and use some of it to butter a 9 inch diameter nonstick cake pan. Lay the first sheet of phyllo pastry inside the pan, letting the excess hang over the sides. Brush the pastry with more melted butter. Repeat with the rest of the sheets, turning the pan a little before layering each additional sheet and brushing the pastry all over with melted butter. When all the pastry is used, transfer the filling into the pan and fold over the excess pastry to cover.

Brush the top with melted butter and bake in the oven for about 25–30 minutes, or until the phyllo is crisp and golden. Let stand for 5 minutes, then turn out and cut into wedges to serve.

Tip

Be sure to butter the phyllo sheets well, so that they will turn crisp and golden in the oven.

This is a serious winter warmer and comforting pie. The rich, soft confit duck flesh is baked in herbs and spices, creating a delicious gravy, and is topped with a creamy mashed potato that will gratinate as it bakes in the oven.

Shredded duck pie

Serves 6

Preparation time: 25 minutes

Cooking time: 1½ hours

1½ lb duck confit, about 4 legs

6 russet or Yukon gold potatoes (1 lb 10 oz), peeled and cut into chunks

⅔ cup milk

2 tablespoons butter

2 tablespoons finely chopped flat-leaf parsley

2 tablespoons vegetable oil

1 onion, finely chopped

2 garlic cloves, crushed

2 celery sticks, chopped

2 teaspoons coarsely chopped rosemary

2 teaspoons chopped thyme

2 tablespoons tomato paste

¼ cup beef stock

salt and freshly ground black pepper

Remove any excess cold fat from the duck legs, then place them on a rack in a deep baking pan. Bake in a preheated oven, at 400°F, for 15–20 minutes, then set aside until cool enough to handle.

When the duck has cooled, remove all the meat from the bones. Coarsely shred it and set aside. Reduce the oven temperature to 350°F.

Cook the potatoes in a large saucepan of boiling salted water until just soft, then drain, return them to the pan, and mash. Heat together the milk and butter in a small saucepan and gently fold into the mashed potatoes. Check the seasoning, add the parsley, and mix thoroughly.

Heat the oil in a heavy skillet. Add the onion and sauté for 3–4 minutes, then add the garlic, celery, rosemary, and thyme and cook for another 3–4 minutes. Add the shredded duck and stir in the tomato paste. Pour the stock over the duck and gently reheat. Check the seasoning and cook for 1–2 minutes.

Transfer the duck mixture to a 2 quart ovenproof dish, about 10½ x 8 x 1¾ inches. Spoon the mashed potatoes in a large pastry bag fitted with a wide star tip, and pipe them on top of the duck in a neat pattern.

Bake the pie in the oven for 35–40 minutes, or until golden. Serve with green beans.

I really liked these closed pizzas when I was in Italy.
I've swapped the pizza dough for the fluffiest brioche,
which lightens up the recipe.

Calzone

Serves 6

Preparation time: 20 minutes,
plus cooling

Cooking time: 50 minutes

2 tablespoons olive oil,
plus extra for greasing

1 onion, finely chopped

2 garlic cloves, crushed

3 tomatoes, peeled and
finely chopped

bunch of fresh basil,
coarsely chopped

10 oz lean ground beef

3½ oz chorizo, chopped

1 (2 oz) can anchovies,
drained and chopped

1¾ cups shredded
mozzarella cheese

about ½ quantity (1 lb) brioche
pastry dough (see page 14)

all-purpose flour, for dusting

2 egg yolks, beaten

1 oz Parmesan cheese

freshly ground black pepper

Heat the olive oil in a skillet. Add the onion and garlic and cook
until softened. Add the chopped tomatoes and cook for another
5 minutes. Stir in the basil, beef, chorizo, and anchovies. Cover and
cook over low heat for 10–15 minutes, then let cool.

Meanwhile, preheat the oven to 425°F. Grease and flour 2 large
baking sheets.

Add the mozzarella to the cooled mixture (if there is a bit too much
liquid, drain it away before adding the cheese), then season with
only pepper.

On a floured surface, roll out the dough about ¼ inch thick and
cut out 6 oval shapes, then transfer them to the baking sheets. Brush
the pastry edges with some of the beaten egg yolk. Spoon the filling
onto the pastry shapes, leaving a 1 inch border, then fold the pastry over
the filling like a turnover and press the edges together to seal. Brush
all over the top of the calzone with the rest of the egg yolk, then grate
the Parmesan directly over the tops.

Bake in the oven for 20–25 minutes, or until raised and golden.
Serve immediately with a wild arugula salad.

Tip

Brushing the brioche pastry with egg yolk gives the finished calzone a
lovely golden glaze.

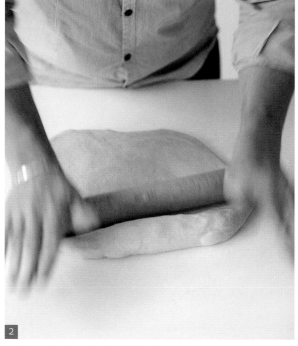

1
Transfer the brioche dough to a floured surface.

Calzone

2
Roll out the dough ¼ inch thick.

5
Spoon the filling onto the pastry.

6
Fold the pastry over the filling.

7
Press the edges together to seal.

3

Cut out 6 oval shapes.

4

Transfer to baking sheets and brush the edges with egg yolk.

8

Brush all over with egg yolk to glaze.

9

Grate Parmesan over the top before baking.

These mini pies are perfect as appetizers or for party food. Only the white crabmeat is used, which makes them really delicious and flavorsome.

Thai crab mini pies

Serves 6

Preparation time: 20 minutes

Cooking time: 15 minutes

2 eggs

⅔ cup heavy cream

3 red chiles, seeded and finely chopped

1¼ inch piece of fresh ginger root, peeled and grated

2 teaspoons lemon grass paste

8 small scallions, finely chopped

1 tablespoon chopped fresh cilantro

8 oz white crabmeat (preferably fresh)

6 individual prebaked flaky pastry shells (see page 10), each in individual 4 inch diameter pie plates or large 1¼ cup ramekins

2 sheets of phyllo pastry

4 tablespoons butter, melted

salt and freshly ground black pepper

Preheat the oven to 350°F.

Beat the eggs in a large bowl, then beat in the cream, chiles, ginger, lemon grass paste, scallions, and cilantro. Season with salt and pepper. Dry the crabmeat on paper towels and divide it among the cooked pastry shells. Pour the cream mixture over the crab, being careful not to overfill the shells.

Brush the phyllo pastry with the melted butter and cut each sheet into 6 squares. Scrunch the squares up and place one on top of each pie to cover. Bake in the oven for 15–20 minutes, or until the pies are nice and golden.

Serve hot in the dishes, with a herb salad of fresh cilantro and pomegranate seeds with a sesame seed dressing.

Tip

You can buy prepared lemon grass paste in some large supermarkets and Asian grocery stores, or you can make your own by blending fresh lemon grass in a food processor until it forms a fine paste.

This recipe requires a little preparation the day before, but it is worth it, because it is such a succulent dish.

Miso cod in brioche pie

Serves 4

Preparation time: 20 minutes, plus marinating

Cooking time: 30 minutes

4 (5 oz) cod fillet pieces (black if possible)

butter, for greasing

all-purpose flour, for dusting

about ½ quantity (1 lb) brioche pastry dough (see page 14)

2 egg yolks, beaten

For the miso marinade

⅔ cup sake

1⅔ cups white miso paste

1 cup plus 2 tablespoons sugar

To make the marinade, bring the sake to a boil in a large saucepan and stir in the miso paste. Add the sugar and stir until dissolved. Let cool. Place the cod fillets in a flat dish and cover with the miso marinade. Cover with plastic wrap and place in the refrigerator for 24 hours.

Preheat the oven to 400°F. Grease a large baking sheet.

On a floured surface, roll out the dough to a large rectangular shape about ¼ inch thick and brush off any extra flour. Brush the upper surface of the pastry with some of the beaten egg yolk. Remove the cod from the marinade, shaking off the excess, but do not dry. Place the cod fillets tightly together in the center of the pastry. Carefully bring the sides of the pastry over the cod to enclose it like a package. Reserve the marinade for the dressing.

Transfer the package to the baking sheet, making sure the seam is underneath, and brush with the rest of the egg yolk. Using a sharp knife, make a few incisions in the top.

Bake in the oven for 30 minutes, or until the pastry is nicely raised and golden and the fish has cooked inside.

To make a dressing, pour the reserved miso marinade into a small saucepan over medium heat and cook for 5 minutes, until it has reduced to a syrup consistency.

Once cooked, serve the cod immediately with steamed baby bok choy and the reduced miso marinade dressing.

Tip

Miso is a Japanese fermented paste made from soybeans and rice, barley, wheat, or rye. It provides a savory, rich flavor.

Quick savory bakes

Recipe ideas using store-bought pastry dough

Fig and pancetta tarts serves 6

Roll out a sheet of store-bought puff pastry until it's really thin (about ⅛ inch) or large enough to fit on a nonstick baking sheet. Top with 4 oz of scrunched-up pancetta and 3 or 4 quartered figs. Add a handful of thyme leaves, plenty of salt and pepper, and a light drizzle of balsamic glaze for a contrasting sharpness, which will complement and bring out the sweet flavor of the figs. Bake in a preheated oven, at 350°F, for 10–12 minutes, or until crisp. Cut into squares and serve with a lightly dressed arugula salad.

Tapenade rolls serves 12

Cut a sheet of store-bought puff pastry in half to make 2 long strips. Spread a thin layer of tapenade over each strip of pastry. Roll each strip up to make 2 long rolls and slice into pinwheels. Place on nonstick baking sheets, brush with beaten egg, and sprinkle with sesame seeds. Bake in a preheated oven, at 350°F, for 8–10 minutes, or until golden. These are perfect for serving with drinks. Alternatively, try making these with pesto or sun-dried tomato paste.

Parmesan pastry soup toppers serves 12

Roll out a sheet of store-bought puff pastry until it's really thin (about ⅛ inch). Brush with beaten egg and use a pastry cutter to cut out 2 inch discs. Place them on nonstick baking sheets, sprinkle 1 cup grated Parmesan cheese among the circles, and bake in a preheated oven, at 350°F, for about 10 minutes, or until crisp and golden. Use to top mugs or bowls of steaming hot soup—delicious!

Quick calzone serves 4

Sauté a thinly sliced onion with 4 oz sliced chorizo in a little olive oil until the onion has started to soften. Roll out a sheet of store-bought puff pastry until it's really thin (about 1/8 inch) and cut into 4 squares. Place the pastry squares on a nonstick baking sheet and brush a 1/2 inch border around the pastry with beaten egg. Spread a teaspoon of tomato paste in the corner of each square and top with the cooked onion and chorizo. Add an anchovy and 1 cup shredded mozzarella or cheddar cheese. Fold over the corner of the pastry to make a triangle, enclosing the filling and seal the edges. Brush the top with beaten egg and bake in a preheated oven, at 350°F, for 15 minutes or until golden.

Caramelized onion and goat cheese pastries serves 4

Cut out 4 circles from a sheet of store-bought flaky pastry dough and place them on 2 nonstick baking sheets. Brush with beaten egg and spread 1 tablespoon caramelized red onion chutney over the circles. Top with a slice of beefsteak tomato, a few basil leaves, and a slice of goat cheese. Season with salt and pepper and bake in a preheated oven, at 350°F, for 12–15 minutes, or until golden.

Quick fish pie serves 4

Take 2 sheets of store-bought puff pastry, lay 1 sheet on a large baking sheet, and brush a 1/2 inch border around the pastry with beaten egg. In a bowl, mix 1 cup cream cheese with 2/3 cup cooked chopped spinach, 1/2 teaspoon grated nutmeg, and 2 beaten eggs. Season with salt and pepper, then spread the mixture inside the border of the pastry. Top with 12 oz diced uncooked fish, such as salmon, cod, or haddock, and 4 oz cooked, peeled shrimp. Top with the other pastry sheet and seal the edges. Brush with beaten egg and make a hole in the top to let steam escape. Bake in a preheated oven, at 350°F, for about 30 minutes, or until puffed up and golden.

Savory accompaniments

Green beans with shallots   serves 6

One of my favorite side dishes—al dente green beans, zesty shallots, and the lovely crunch of roasted hazelnuts.

2½ cups trimmed green beans
3½ cups broccoli florets
2 shallots, chopped finely
2 teaspoons red wine vinegar
½ cup roasted hazelnuts, chopped
salt and freshly ground black pepper

Put the beans and broccoli into a saucepan of boiling water with a couple of pinches of salt and cook until al dente. Drain the vegetables and plunge them into icy water to keep their bright green color.

When ready to serve, drain the beans and broccoli and place in a serving bowl. Mix the chopped shallots in a bowl with the vinegar and season with salt and pepper. Pour this over the greens and sprinkle with the chopped hazelnuts.

Tomato salsa   serves 6

The perfect summery accompaniment, full of flavor and bright in color and versatile.

4 tomatoes, peeled and cut into small dice
1 red onion, finely chopped
1 red chile, seeded and minced
1 tablespoon chopped fresh cilantro
grated zest and juice of 1 lime

Put the tomato, onion, and chile into a bowl and mix together, then add the chopped cilantro and the lemon zest and juice. Chill for 30 minutes before serving.

Moroccan roasted vegetables   serves 6

This is ideal to serve with meat pie recipes, and especially good with lamb.

1 large sweet potato (8 oz), peeled and cut into large chunks
¼ butternut squash, peeled and cut into large chunks
1 garlic clove, finely chopped
2 tablespoons olive oil
1 cup Greek yogurt
3 teaspoons ras el hanout

Place the sweet potato, butternut squash, and garlic on a baking sheet and drizzle with the oil. Roast in a preheated oven, at 350°F, for 40 minutes, until soft. Once cooked, put on a serving dish, pile the yogurt on top, and sprinkle with the spice before serving.

Middle Eastern tabouleh salad   serves 6

A refreshing side salad to serve with a summery recipe.

1 firm tomato, chopped
½ a red onion, chopped
juice of 1 lemon
½ teaspoon cayenne pepper (optional)
3 bunches of flat-leaf parsley, finely chopped
small bunch of mint, chopped
½ tablespoon extra virgin olive oil
salt and freshly ground black pepper

Put the tomatoes, onions, and lemon juice into a large bowl and mix well. Season with salt and pepper, and add the cayenne, if using.

Add the chopped parsley and mint, then the olive oil, and mix, adjusting the seasoning by adding more oil and lemon, if desired.

Onion marmalade   serves 6

This rich marmalade is great served with some of the more hearty recipes in this book, such as the beet tart on page 51.

¼ cup white vinegar
1/3 cup firmly packed dark brown sugar
grated zest and juice of 1 large orange
2 tsp ground allspice
6 large red onions, sliced
2 cups fresh cranberries (or frozen)

Put the vinegar and brown sugar into a heavy saucepan and add the orange zest and juice and the allspice. Bring to a simmer and cook until reduced down by one-third.

Add the sliced onions and cranberries and reduce by one-hird again. Let cool, then serve.

Fig chutney   serves 6

This chutney is made with dried figs, which give it a luscious honey flavor and great texture, too.

1½ cups dried figs
1 red onion, sliced
2 teaspoons olive oil
2/3 cup light brown sugar
1 cup white wine vinegar
½ teaspoon ground ginger
½ teaspoon ground nutmeg
salt and freshly ground black pepper
Plunge the figs into a saucepan of boiling water and let simmer for 15 minutes, then drain.

Sauté the onion in the oil until soft. Add the sugar and let it caramelize slightly, then add the figs, vinegar, and spices. Let simmer over low heat for 1 hour, making sure it doesn't burn.

Let cool, then store in a covered, sterilized jar for up to 4 weeks in the refrigerator.

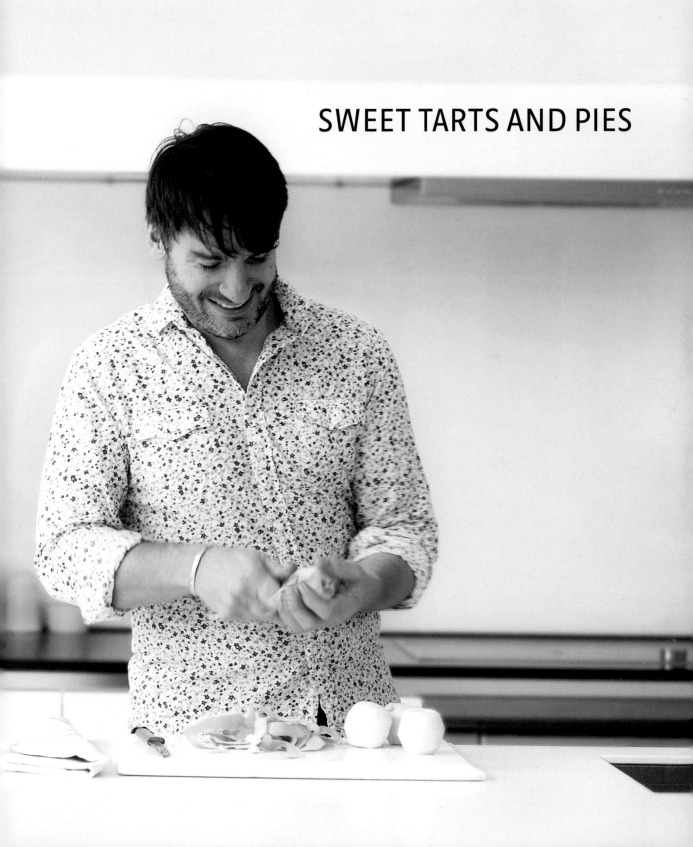

SWEET TARTS AND PIES

Sweet

One of the most exciting things about baking sweet tarts and pies is the pleasure I get from making all the different varieties of lovely pastry. From light, crumbly sweet flaky pastry to fluffy, buttery brioche or rich puff, a good pie or tart will be first judged by the quality of the pastry—even if the filling is delicious, a bad pastry can ruin the overall effect. You can easily raise the level of your baking by using alternative flavors, such as my indulgent Almond flaky pastry (see page 11), or rich Chocolate pastry (see page 12) which will complement any recipe with cocoa. Sometimes just the addition of nuts or fresh herbs, such as mint, to the pastry will boost the flavor or the texture of the recipe.

I've combined here a selection of delicious, exciting, and updated sweet tarts and pies, from Old-fashioned apple pie to a rich Southern chocolate mud pie and the more unusual Mango and green peppercorn pie. I am sure you will find much to inspire you and to fit any occasion, from casual dining to a big family celebration. Some of these recipes are bound to become your classics, too.

This tart is inspired by my trips to the Middle East. I love Middle Eastern sweets, with their crusty and flaky pastry dripping with honey or fragrant syrup. This tart is rustic and made to share.

Apricot, honey, and pistachio tart

Serves 6

Preparation time: 25 minutes

Cooking time: 40 minutes

1 stick unsalted butter, melted

6 sheets of phyllo pastry

11 fresh apricots (1 lb), halved and pitted

⅓ cup firmly packed light brown sugar

¼ cup honey

3 tablespoons coarsely chopped shelled pistachio nuts

1–2 tablespoons confectioners' sugar

For the filling

1 stick unsalted butter, softened

⅔ cup superfine sugar

⅔ cup ground almonds (almond meal)

⅔ cup ground pistachio nuts

4 drops of almond extract

1 teaspoon pure vanilla paste or extract

3 eggs

Start by making the filling. Cream together the butter and the superfine sugar until pale and fluffy. Add the ground almonds and ground pistachios and beat until nice and smooth. Add the almond extract and vanilla and beat in the eggs one at a time.

Preheat your oven to 350°F. With a pastry brush, use a little of the melted butter to grease the inside of an 8½ inch diameter, 1 inch deep tart pan or baking pan.

Separate the sheets of phyllo pastry, covering those you are not using with a damp cloth to prevent them from drying out. Brush some melted butter across 1 sheet of phyllo and cover the bottom and sides of the pan, leaving about 3 inch of the pastry hanging over the edge of the pan. Repeat this operation with another 4 sheets, laying the pastry in a crisscross pattern to cover the bottom and inside of the pan.

Carefully spread the pistachio cream evenly in the bottom about ¾ inch deep. Place the apricots in an informal way on top of the cream (this is a rustic tart!). Sprinkle the brown sugar over the apricots. Fold the pastry edges over the filling. Butter the remaining phyllo sheet, scrunch it up, and top the tart, covering the filling.

Bake in the oven for 40–45 minutes, or until the pastry is golden and caramelized and the apricots are soft. Place the tart, still in its pan, on a cooling rack and drizzle all over with the honey. Let cool before removing from the pan. Sprinkle chopped pistachio nuts over the tart, lightly dust with confectioners' sugar, and serve warm, with a generous serving of Greek yogurt flavored with vanilla, honey, and rose water.

Tip

If fresh apricots are not available, you can substitute canned apricots.

The Caribbean is one of my favorite vacation destinations. Grenada is called the spice island, and it grows some amazing spices as well as cacao. In this recipe, I've combined these fabulous local ingredients. It's a decadent exotic dessert ... with a crunch!

West Indies chocolate tart

Serves 8

Preparation time: 20 minutes, plus chilling

Cooking time: 20 minutes

1 cup light cream

3 tablespoons glucose syrup

1 vanilla bean, split

1 star anise

1 cinnamon stick

½ teaspoon freshly grated nutmeg

7 oz semisweet dark chocolate, broken into pieces

6 tablespoons unsalted butter

1 prebaked chocolate flaky pastry shell (see page 12), in an 8½ inch square, 1¼ inch deep tart pan

For the nougatine

¼ cup milk

1 stick unsalted butter, chopped

3 tablespoons glucose syrup

¾ cup superfine sugar

¾ cup toasted slivered almonds

⅓ cup coffee beans, crushed

To decorate

cinnamon sticks, star anise and unsweetened cocoa powder

Put the cream, glucose, vanilla bean, and spices into a saucepan and bring to a boil. Remove from the heat and set aside to steep for 10 minutes.

Place the chocolate in a large bowl. Pour the flavored cream through a strainer over the chocolate. While the mixture is warm, add the butter and stir gently using a wooden spoon until blended—it should melt in the residual heat. Don't overstir. Pour the mixture into the cooked pastry shell and let set in the refrigerator.

Preheat the oven to 350°F. Line a baking sheet with silicone paper.

To make the nougatine, put the milk, butter, and glucose into a clean saucepan and heat gently until the butter has melted. Add the sugar and stir until dissolved. Increase the heat until you have a thick syrup, but not a caramel (to 222°F on a sugar thermometer, if you have one). Remove from the heat and stir in the slivered almonds and crushed coffee beans. Pour the mixture onto the prepared baking sheet and bake in the oven for 12–15 minutes, or until the nougatine has turned a nice caramel color.

Let the nougatine cool until brittle. Break into large pieces and decorate the tart by pushing pieces of nougatine into the set filling. Then decorate with cinnamon sticks and star anise, and, finally, with a generous dusting of cocoa powder.

A rich crème anglaise (see page 169) flavored with vanilla seeds and dark rum will be perfect with this indulgence!

Tip

Glucose syrup is available in the baking sections of some large supermarkets, in pharmacies, and online, in either tubes or small jars.

These individual chocolate tarts are perfect as a yummy dessert that tastes and looks spectacular. The heat of the freshly roasted figs starts melting the chocolate ganache filling, making these creations very delicious and indulgent.

Chocolate and Earl Grey tarts with roasted figs

Serves 6

Preparation time: 10 minutes, plus steeping

Cooking time: 15 minutes

2 cups light cream

2 Earl Grey teabags

10 oz semisweet dark chocolate

6 prebaked chocolate flaky pastry shells, each in individual 4 inch diameter tart pans, using about ½ quantity (8 oz) dough (see page 12)

6 large figs (or 12 small ones)

2 tablespoons firmly packed light brown sugar

1 teaspoon ground cinnamon

Put the cream into a saucepan and bring to a boil. Remove from the heat and add the teabags. Let steep for at least 30 minutes.

Melt the chocolate in a heatproof bowl set over a saucepan of simmering water, making sure the water does not touch the surface of the bowl.

When the teabags have steep the cream, remove them and squeeze out the liquid. Reheat the cream but do not let it boil. Pass it through a fine strainer onto the warm chocolate and mix gently until smooth and glossy. Fill the cooked pastry shells to the top and let set in the refrigerator for 1 hour.

Preheat the oven to 350°F.

Cut the figs into quarters—don't cut all the way through so that the quarters remain joined at the bottom, then place on a baking sheet. Sprinkle with the sugar and cinnamon and roast in the oven for 10–12 minutes, or until the figs become soft and the lovely juices start to ooze out.

Using a large spoon, arrange the figs on top of the set tarts. Drizzle with some of the hot juice and serve immediately with a spoonful of cinnamon-flavored crème fraîche.

Tip

For a touch of glamour, lightly dust the figs with confectioners' sugar and gold edible glitter just before serving.

After my apprenticeship in Brittany, I went to work for a year in Luxembourg. The standard of the pâtisserie was high and one of the specialities was streusel tart. The black currant version was my favorite because it was very tangy. I just love the way the juices ooze through the crunchy topping.

Black currant streusel tart

Serves 8
Preparation time: 25 minutes
Cooking time: 35 minutes

1 quantity (14½ oz) sweet flaky pastry dough (see page 11)

butter, for greasing

all-purpose flour, for dusting

3½ cups fresh or frozen black currants

½ cup superfine sugar

1 teaspoon grated lemon zest and 1 tablespoon lemon juice

2 tablespoons fine semolina

2 teaspoons black currant syrup

For the crème pâtissière

6 egg yolks

½ cup superfine sugar

3 tablespoons cornstarch

1½ cups milk

1 vanilla bean, split lengthwise

For the streusel topping

1 cup whole-wheat flour

¼ cup packed light brown sugar

4 tablespoons unsalted butter

½ teaspoon ground cinnamon

½ cup ground almonds (almond meal)

Preheat the oven to 350°F. Grease a 9 inch diameter, 1¼ inch deep, loose-bottom tart pan. Roll out the dough on a lightly floured surface and use it to line the pan (see page 18).

To make the crème pâtissière, whisk together the egg yolks and sugar in a large bowl until pale and fluffy. Add the cornstarch and mix well. Put the milk and vanilla bean into a large saucepan and bring to a boil. Remove the vanilla bean and pour the steeped milk over the egg mixture, whisking all the time. Pour the mixture back into the saucepan and stir over low heat until it comes to a gentle boil. Cook for 2 minutes. Remove from the heat and let cool, then spread over the bottom of the pastry shell.

Next make the black currant filling by mixing together the black currants, superfine sugar, lemon zest and juice, semolina, and black currant syrup in a bowl. Spread this over the crème pâtissière.

Finally, make the streusel topping by placing all the ingredients in a large bowl. Using the tips of your fingers, rub in the butter until you get a rough crumb mixture. Cover the tart completely with the streusel.

Bake in the oven for 30–35 minutes, or until the topping is nice and golden and the juices from the fruits start to bubble away. Let cool before removing from the tart pan.

I like serving mine warm with a Champagne sabayon, which has almost all the flavor of a kir royale in a dessert!

When I was a child my family and I would sometimes escape the unpredictable weather of Brittany to spend a week in southwest France, and the Pyrenees was our favorite destination. Guaranteed sun, without all the bustle of the south ... and where peach trees line the roads. This recipe brings back so many good memories for me.

Amaretto and peach tart

Serves 8

Preparation time: 20 minutes, plus marinating overnight

Cooking time: 45 minutes

6 ripe peaches (but not too soft)

1 cup water

2 cups superfine sugar

2 vanilla beans, split lengthwise

1 stick unsalted butter, softened

2⅔ cups ground almonds (almond meal)

2 eggs

2 tablespoons amaretto liqueur

1 prebaked almond flaky pastry shell, in a 9 inch diameter, 1¼ inch deep tart pan, using about ½ quantity (10 oz) of pastry (see page 11)

½ cup slivered almonds

The day before you want to make the tart, boil enough water in a large saucepan to cover the peaches. Add the peaches and blanch them for 2 minutes, then drain and rinse in cold water. Use a sharp knife to remove the skins.

Put the water, 1 cup of the superfine sugar, and the vanilla beans into a saucepan and bring to a boil. Boil for 5 minutes, then reduce the heat to a slight simmer, add the peaches, and poach them for 10 minutes. Remove the pan from the heat and let the peaches cool in the syrup. Cover and let steep overnight in the refrigerator.

When you are ready to cook the tart, preheat the oven to 350°F.

In a large bowl, cream together the butter, remaining sugar, and the ground almonds. Beat in the eggs, one at a time, then fold in the amaretto. Spread the mixture over the bottom of the cooked pastry shell.

Remove the poached peaches from the syrup and slice them, removing the pits. Fan them out on top of the almond cream. Sprinkle the slivered almonds over the top and bake in the oven for 30–35 minutes or until the tart is golden.

Let cool in the pan and serve with a pure almond milk sorbet.

Tip

Always make sure the ground almonds you use for pastry are fresh.

You know summer has arrived when strawberries and bright red stems of rhubarb are piled high at your local farmers' market. This tart is so refreshing and tangy, especially with the fresh mint-flavored pastry.

Rhubarb and strawberry tart

Serves 6–8

Preparation time: 20 minutes, plus cooling

Cooking time: 10 minutes

1 quantity (14¼ oz) sweet flaky pastry dough (see page 11), with the chopped leaves from a bunch of mint added

1 tablespoon lemon juice

1 tablespoon cornstarch

1 quart strawberries, hulled and halved (about 4½ cups)

3 pink rhubarb stalks, trimmed and cut into ½ inch slices

½ cup granulated sugar mixed with ½ teaspoon powdered pectin for lower-sugar recipes

To decorate

confectioners' sugar

mint sprigs

Grease a 9 inch diameter, 1¼ inch deep, loose-bottom tart pan. Roll the dough out on a lightly floured surface and use the pastry to line the pan (see page 18). Cover the pastry with parchment paper and pie weights or dried beans and prebake (see page 19). Let cool in the pan.

Put the lemon juice and cornstarch into a large saucepan and stir to blend. Add ⅔ cup of the strawberries, all the rhubarb, and the granulated sugar and pectin. Heat gently to dissolve the sugar, then simmer for 10–15 minutes, until it forms a chunky compote—not too runny or watery. Let cool.

It is best to assemble this dessert just before serving to prevent the pastry from becoming soggy. Remove the cooked pastry shell from the pan and spread the cooled compote in the bottom. Arrange the remaining strawberries on top and decorate with sprigs of mint. Dust with confectioners' sugar and serve immediately.

A vanilla ice cream will complement the freshness of this dessert.

Tip

The powdered pectin for lower-sugar recipes helps the compote stay firm. Look for it in the baking aisles in supermarkets or order it online.

Sometimes fresh herbs or spices help to boost the original flavor of ingredients—black pepper with strawberries, salt with chocolate. In this case, I am adding the fresh flavor of basil to enhance the raspberries. I just love the way all the juices of the baked raspberries ooze through the pastry shell.

Baked raspberry and basil tart

Serves: 8

Preparation time: 15 minutes, plus infusing overnight

Cooking time: 20 minutes

1 plain sponge cake, 8 inch in diameter

1 prebaked sweet flaky pastry shell (see page 11), in a 9 inch diameter, 1¼ inch deep tart pan

⅓ cup raspberry preserves

4 cups raspberries

For the basil syrup

½ cup water

⅔ cup superfine sugar

6 basil leaves

To make the basil syrup, put the water and sugar into a saucepan and heat to boiling point. Add the basil and let steep for as long as possible—ideally, overnight.

Preheat the oven to 400°F. Cut the sponge cake in half, horizontally across the center.

Spread one-half of the cake with the raspberry preserves and place it preserves side down in the cooked pastry shell. (Reserve the other half of the sponge cake for another day.)

Remove the basil leaves from the syrup and discard them, then spoon the syrup over the sponge until it is evenly soaked.

Cover the tart with the raspberries and bake in the oven for 15 minutes or until the raspberries are hot and oozing juice. Serve immediately.

Tip

The leftover sponge can be frozen and used for other desserts or to layer a trifle.

This is one of Cake Boy's best-selling tarts. It's also my perfect dessert to finish a rich meal or dinner. The filling is so zesty it will work all your taste buds in one mouthful!

Tarte au citron

Serves 6
Preparation time: 15 minutes
Cooking time: 15 minutes

4 large lemons

¾ cup plus 2 tablespoons sugar

2 eggs

1¾ sticks unsalted butter, diced

1 prebaked sweet flaky pastry shell (see page 11), in a 9 inch diameter, 1¼ inch deep tart pan

2 tablespoons granulated sugar

Grate the zest from 2 of the lemons, then thinly pare the zest from the other 2 and cut into julienne strips. Squeeze the juice from enough lemons to make ⅔ cup. Put the grated zest and lemon juice into a saucepan with ⅓ cup of the sugar and bring to a boil. Set aside the julienne of lemon zest.

In a large bowl, whisk the eggs with the remaining sugar until pale and fluffy. Pour the hot lemon juice over the beaten eggs, whisking continuously. Return the mixture to the saucepan and gradually bring to a gentle boil, then simmer for 2–3 minutes, stirring continuously.

Remove from the heat, add the butter, and gently stir until smooth. Let cool for 10–15 minutes, then pour into the cooked pastry shell. Let cool completely in the refrigerator.

To decorate, make some candied zest. Bring a small saucepan of water to a boil, add the reserved julienne of lemon zest, and boil for 10 minutes. Drain, then roll the strips of zest in the granulated sugar to coat. Decorate the tart with the zest before serving.

I like this tart on its own, but a lot of my friends like a little cream on the side.

This recipe is a French classic and the blueberry (*myrtille*) version is my favorite. Alternatively, it also works very well with raspberries.

Blueberry amandine tarts

Serves 6

Preparation time: 10 minutes

Cooking time: 20 minutes

butter, for greasing

all-purpose flour, for dusting

1 quantity (14½ oz) sweet flaky pastry dough (see page 11)

1¾ cups fresh or frozen blueberries

2 eggs

⅔ cup crème fraîche

⅓ cup superfine sugar

½ cup ground almonds (almond meal)

1 tablespoon cornstarch

1 drop of almond extract

2 tablespoons slivered almonds

Preheat the oven to 350°F.

Grease 6 individual 4 inch diameter loose-bottom tart pans. Roll out the dough on a lightly floured surface and use it to line the pans (see page 18).

Divide the blueberries among the pastry shells to fill each one three-quarters full.

Break the eggs into a large bowl and mix in the crème fraîche. Add the superfine sugar, ground almonds, cornstarch, and almond extract and stir well until smooth. Pour the mixture over the blueberries, making sure to cover them completely. Sprinkle the slivered almonds over the top. Bake in the oven for 20–25 minutes, or until the pastry is nice and golden.

Let cool in the pans, then serve warm or cold with crème fraîche.

Tip

A shiny glaze will add a professional finish to these tarts; gently warm 2 tablepoons apricot preserves in a small saucepan, then strain and brush on top of each tart before baking.

Tarte Bourdaloue is a classic dish, and this is my take on it. I've replaced the almonds with hazelnuts, giving a more nutty taste and the dark chocolate drizzle is the perfect finish.

Pear and hazelnut tart

Serves 8–10

Preparation time: overnight for the pears, plus 25 minutes, plus chilling

Cooking time: 15 minutes

1 prebaked sweet flaky pastry shell (see page 11), in a 9 inch square, 1¼ inch deep tart pan

2½ oz semisweet dark chocolate, chopped

¼ cup roasted hazelnuts (or almonds), coarsely chopped

For the poached pears

8 large pears

½ cup water

½ cup superfine sugar

1 vanilla bean, split lengthwise

For the hazelnut cream

1¼ cups milk

½ cup cornstarch

3 eggs

2 teaspoons vanilla sugar

⅓ cup superfine sugar

scant 1¼ cups roasted ground hazelnuts

The day before you are planning to make the tart, poach the pears. Peel them, cut them in half, and remove the cores. Put the water, sugar, and vanilla bean into a large saucepan. Gradually bring to a boil, stirring until the sugar dissolves. Plunge the pears into the simmering syrup, cover, and cook for 10–12 minutes, or until a knife goes into the flesh easily. Remove the pan from the heat and let the pears cool in the syrup, then place the pears, still in the saucepan, in the refrigerator overnight for the flavors to meld.

When you are ready to make the tart, make the hazelnut cream. Pour the milk into a saucepan and bring it to a boil. Put the cornstarch into a large bowl and mix in the eggs, one at a time. Add the sugars and mix well. Pour the hot milk over the egg mixture and stir well. Return the mixture to the saucepan and bring to a boil, then simmer for 2 minutes, stirring continuously.

Add the ground hazelnuts to the cream and mix well until combined. Using a spatula, spread the cream into the cooked pastry shell.

Melt the chocolate in a bowl over a saucepan of barely simmering water, making sure the bottom of the bowl does not touch the surface of the water. Drain the pear halves and arrange them on top of the cream, sprinkle with the roasted hazelnuts, and drizzle with the melted chocolate to finish. Let cool in the refrigerator for a minimum of 2 hours before serving.

Tip

I like to roast the hazelnuts for a few minutes in a hot oven to enhance their flavor.

Sometimes the simplest things are the best, and this recipe is the perfect example! Flaky, buttery pastry, crunchy but cooked apple, and the final taste of the roasted almond and honey glaze—it's a perfect dessert, and one that can be made quickly.

Tarte aux pommes

Serves 6–8

Preparation time: 15 minutes

Cooking time: 30 minutes

8 oz store-bought or ¼ quantity homemade puff pastry (see page 16)

all-purpose flour, for dusting

1 egg yolk, lightly beaten

4½ tablespoons lightly salted butter, melted

½ cup firmly packed light brown sugar

6 Granny Smith or Pippin apples, cored, peeled, and thinly sliced

⅔ cup slivered almonds

2 tablespoons honey

Preheat the oven to 400°F/.

Roll the puff pastry into a 10½ inch diameter circle on a lightly floured surface. Carefully lift the pastry circle onto a large baking sheet. With a little water, wet the edge of the pastry using a pastry brush. Using your fingers, roll up the edges of the pastry just a little to make a border. Brush the border with the egg yolk and brush the rest of the pastry generously with half the melted butter. Sprinkle the buttered pastry with the sugar.

Arrange the apple slices in a fan pattern, covering the tart and overlapping the border. Brush the apples with the rest of the melted butter and sprinkle over the slivered almonds. Bake in the oven for 20 minutes, or until the pastry is nice and golden and the apples start to color on the edges.

Warm the honey in a small saucepan and drizzle it all over the hot apples. Return the tart to the oven for another 10 minutes to let the honey caramelize. Serve immediately—my favorite accompaniment is a salted butter caramel ice cream or sauce.

Tip

An easy way to lift the pastry circle is to roll the pastry dough out on top of a large sheet of plastic wrap, then use the plastic wrap to lift the pastry and drape it over your rolling pin. Lay the pastry over the baking sheet and simply peel off the plastic wrap.

I remember my mom baking this tart using the leftover nougat we used to get in bulk during the Christmas period. The combination of the nuts and the sweet honey taste of the nougat works very well with the chunky apple slices.

Apple and almond nougat tart

Serves 8

Preparation time: 15 minutes

Cooking time: 30 minutes

2 eggs

¼ cup superfine sugar

1 tablespoon cornstarch

⅔ cup milk

1 tablespoon heavy cream

3½ oz nougat

3 Granny Smith or Pippin apples, peeled, cored, and chopped into chunky slices

1 prebaked sweet flaky pastry shell (see page 11), in a 9 inch diameter, 1¼ inch deep tart pan

⅓ cup golden raisins

3 tablespoons chopped, shelled pistachio nuts

Preheat the oven to 325°F.

Put the eggs and sugar into a large bowl and cream together until pale and creamy. Beat in the cornstarch.

Put the milk, cream, and nougat into a saucepan and bring to a boil. Stir until the nougat has melted. Pour it over the egg mixture and mix well with a whisk.

Arrange the apple slices in the cooked pastry shell and spinkle with the golden raisins and pistachio nuts. Pour the nougat custard over the apples and bake in the oven for 30–35 minutes, or until set and golden.

Tip

Firm eating apples are best for this kind of apple dessert.

Gypsy tart originates from Kent, in the southern part of the UK. This old classic recipe has had a big revival and needs only a few ingredients. I had my first gypsy tart at my friend Mark Sargeant's restaurant, Rocksalt.

Gypsy tart

Serves 8

Preparation time: 15 minutes, plus chilling

Cooking time: 15 minutes

1⅔ cups evaporated milk, chilled

1⅓ cups firmly packed dark brown sugar

1 prebaked sweet flaky pastry shell (see page 11), in a 10 inch diameter, 1¾ inch deep tart pan

Preheat the oven to 350°F.

Put the evaporated milk and sugar in a large bowl and beat, using an electric handheld mixer, for at least 15 minutes, until thick and fluffy.

Pour the mixture into the cooked pastry shell and bake in the oven for 15 minutes. It will come out sticky, but it will set when cold.

Chill for 2 hours, then serve with a generous serving of lemon cheese (see page 167).

Tip

Store the evaporated milk in the refrigerator overnight before using—this will give you an even fluffier filling!

This grand recipe is an old classic that has almost disappeared from the chef's repertoire. It's such a shame, because the combination is extraordinary and it really works.

Strawberry tart "royale"

Serves 8

Preparation time: 15 minutes

Cooking time: 25 minutes

12 oz store-bought puff pastry or about ⅓ quantity homemade puff pastry (see page 16)

all-purpose flour, for dusting

1 tablespoon unsalted butter, melted

4 tablespoons unsalted butter

2 tablespoons firmly packed dark brown sugar

2 bananas (not too ripe), sliced

2 tablespoons banana cream liqueur

1¼ cups heavy whipping cream

2 teaspoons vanilla paste or extract

1¼ cups superfine sugar

1 pint fresh strawberries, hulled and halved (about 2⅓ cups)

Preheat the oven to 400°F.

Roll out the pastry to ¼ inch thick on a lightly floured surface. Cut out a circle about 9 inches in diameter and place on a baking sheet.

Brush the pastry with the melted butter and prick with a fork, leaving a border of ¾ inch around the edge. Cover with a sheet of parchment paper and place a second baking sheet on top. Bake in the oven for 15 minutes, then carefully remove the top baking sheet and the parchment paper and bake for another 5 minutes, or until it is nice and golden. Let cool on the baking sheet on a cooling rack.

Melt together the butter and brown sugar in a skillet over gentle heat. Increase the heat, add the banana slices, and sauté until golden, turning them over once. Drizzle over the liqueur, flambé (flame the alcohol, see tip on page 31), then turn off the heat and let cool in the pan.

Put the whipping cream into a large bowl with the vanilla and ½ cup of the superfine sugar, then beat to form firm peaks.

Place the circle of cooked puff pastry on a serving dish. Cover the center with the cooled banana slices. Using a spatula, spread the cream over the bananas. Arrange the strawberries over the cream.

Put the remaining superfine sugar into a heavy saucepan and heat until caramelized to a golden color. Remove from the heat and drizzle it carefully over the strawberries. I like to decorate my tart with few flakes of edible gold leaf.

Tip

Smear a little of the whipped cream underneath the cooked pastry to stop it from sliding around your serving dish.

1

Roll out the puff pastry, cut out a circle, and bake in the oven.

2

Strawberry tart "royale"

Melt butter with dark brown sugar in a skillet.

5

Smear a little cream on a serving dish to stop the pastry from sliding around.

6

Cover the pastry with the cooked and cooled bananas.

7

Spread cream on top of the bananas.

Flambé the bananas, then let cool.

Add banana slices, cook until golden, then add the banana liqueur.

Arrange the strawberries on top.

Caramelize the superfine sugar in a hot pan and drizzle slowly over the top.

I discovered this British classic more than twenty years ago, when I arrived in the UK. It has had a great revival with the popularity of the "gastro pub", and what used to be a "school dinner pudding" (similar to shoofly pie), is now a fine dessert.

Treacle tart

Serves 6

Preparation time: 10 minutes

Cooking time: 30 minutes

butter, for greasing

about 1 quantity (12 oz) sweet flaky pastry dough (see page 11)

4 thick slices of white bread (without crusts)

finely grated zest and juice of 1 lemon

½ cup golden syrup (available at larger supermarkets and online)

1 teaspoon vanilla extract

Preheat the oven to 400°F. Butter a 10 x 8 inch rectangular tart pan, 1¼ inch deep.

Roll out the pastry on a lightly floured surface and use to line the pan (see page 18). Let rest for at least 12 minutes in the refrigerator.

Crumble the bread into a bowl (I like mine to be a chunky crumb) and add the grated lemon zest. Put the golden syrup into a small saucepan with the lemon juice and vanilla extract and warm over gentle heat. Pour this over the bread crumbs and stir to combine.

Gently spread the mixture in the pastry shell. Bake in the oven for 20 minutes, then reduce the heat to 350°F and bake for another 10 minutes. Let cool completely before removing from the pan.

I like to be very indulgent when serving my treacle tart and accompany it with another British classic, pure Devonshire clotted cream, but crème frâiche, found in larger supermarkets, is delicious with it, too.

Another French classic and my grandmother's speciality ... or should I say almost? She used to cook this dessert in a shallow cast-iron dish, but I am swapping it for a pastry shell to make it easier to serve. You can use canned cherries if fresh ones are out of season.

Cherry clafoutis tart

Serves 6–8

Preparation time: 15 minutes

Cooking time: 20 minutes

1 egg

2 egg yolks

2 tablespoons superfine sugar

2 tablespoons kirsch

scant 1 cup heavy cream

1 teaspoon vanilla extract

1 prebaked sweet flaky pastry shell (see page 11), in a 9 inch diameter, 1¼ inch deep tart pan

1⅔ cups fresh pitted cherries, or canned cherries, well drained

Preheat the oven to 300°F.

Place the egg and yolks in a large heatproof bowl. Add the sugar and kirsch. Place the bowl over a saucepan of barely simmering water, making sure the surface of the water does not touch the bottom of the bowl and whisk the mixture until it becomes light and very fluffy—this may take 10–15 minutes.

Heat the cream with the vanilla extract in a separate saucepan. Gently whisk the hot cream into the egg mixture, then remove from the heat.

Place the cooked pastry shell, still in its pan, on the oven shelf and pour the cream mixture into the pastry shell. Arrange the cherries evenly over the tart, carefully slide into the oven, and bake for 15–20 minutes, or until set and golden. Let cool in the pan, then place in the refrigerator until ready to serve. I like to serve it with spiced cherries (see page 167).

Tip

It's important to drain the cherries really well if you use canned ones.

This Asian-inspired recipe is very refreshing, and the yuzu gives it an unusual and pleasant citrus flavor that works well with the green tea.

Matcha and yuzu tart

Serves 8

Preparation time: 15 minutes, plus chilling

Cooking time: 40 minutes

½ cup confectioners' sugar

¼ cup ground almonds (almond meal)

2½ tablespoons Matcha (green tea powder)

scant 1¼ cups all-purpose flour, plus extra for dusting

5 tablespoons unsalted butter, chopped into pieces

1 egg, lightly beaten

For the yuzu curd

¾ cup plus 2 tablepoons yuzu juice

grated zest of 2 limes

1 cup superfine sugar

1 tablespoon cornstarch

4 eggs

4 tablespons unsalted butter, cut into small cubes

To decorate

strawberries

red currant stems (optional)

confectioners' sugar

Put the confectioners' sugar, ground almonds, Matcha, and flour into a bowl and mix together. Add the butter and rub in using your fingertips. Add the egg and knead until smooth. Cover the dough and let rest in the refrigerator for at least 1 hour.

Preheat the oven to 350°F. Butter and flour a 9 inch diameter, 1¼ inch deep tart pan.

Roll out the dough on a lightly floured surface and use to line the tart pan (see page 18). Cover with parchment paper and pie weights or dried beans and prebake in the oven for 15 minutes, then remove the paper and weights and bake for another 5 minutes. Let cool in the pan.

Put all the yuzu curd ingredients into a heatproof bowl and mix together. Place the bowl over a saucepan of barely simmering water, making sure the water does not touch the surface of the bowl and whisk continuously until the mixture thickens—this will take about 15 minutes. Pass the mixture through a fine strainer into another bowl and let cool for 5 minutes before filling the cooked pastry shell.

Smooth over the top with a spatula and put into the refrigerator for at least 2 hours. Dust confectioners' sugar around the edge before serving and decorate with strawberries and red currant stems, if desired. This tangy tart doesn't need any accompaniment.

Tip

Yuzu is a citrus fruit from Asia that looks a bit like a very small grapefruit. You can find this and matcha in Asian supermarkets. Both are best kept frozen in sealed containers after opening.

This recipe is a speciality of Lyon, the gastronomic capital of France. As well as its unusual mix of texture, it also looks fabulous with its bright pink colors.

"Praline rose" tarts

Serves 6

Preparation time: 15 minutes, plus chilling time

Cooking time: 15 minutes

9 oz *praline rose*, plus an extra 3 oz for decorating

1 cup light cream

3 tablespoons confectioners' sugar

6 prebaked sweet flaky pastry shells (see page 11), each in individual 4 inch diameter tart pans

pink edible glitter, to decorate

Using a mortar and pestle, crush the 9 oz of praline finely. Alternatively, put the praline into a plastic food bag and crush by hitting it with a rolling pin.

Place the crushed praline in a large saucepan with the cream and confectioners' sugar. Bring to a boil, stirring, then let simmer for 15 minutes. Pour the mixture evenly into the cooked pastry shells. Let cool, then refrigerate for at least 2 hours.

Coarsely crush the remaining praline and use to decorate the tarts. Finally dust with pink edible glitter. A generous spoonful of crème fraîche will cut through to the sweetness of this classic tart.

Tip

Praline rose are roasted almond pieces coated in a bright pink hard sugar and originate from the Lyon region of France. They are available from French delicatessens and gourmet food websites.

It's funny how we always assume that a crumb topping should be a pale or golden color. I am breaking the rules and making a chocolate crumb topping with baked apple and pear. Chocolate lovers will love it ... and the smell when it's baking is simply amazing.

Chocolate crumb tart

Serves 8

Preparation time: 20 minutes

Cooking time: 50 minutes

2 apples

2 pears

2 tablespoons unsalted butter

1 tablespoon dark rum

⅓ cup firmly packed dark brown sugar

1 stick unsalted butter, softened

⅔ cup superfine sugar

½ cup unsweetened cocoa powder

1⅓ cups ground almonds (almond meal)

3 eggs

1 uncooked chocolate flaky pastry shell (see page 12), in a 9 inch diameter, 1¼ inch deep tart pan

confectioners' sugar and unsweetened cocoa powder, for dusting

For the crumb topping

¾ cup all-purpose flour

¼ cup unsweetened cocoa powder

¼ cup packed light brown sugar

4 tablespoons unsalted butter

Preheat the oven to 325°F.

Peel and core the apples and pears and chop them into cubes. Melt the butter in a skillet and add the fruit, rum, and dark brown sugar. Cook over medium heat until the fruit has colored but is not mushy. Set aside.

In a bowl, cream together the butter, superfine sugar, cocoa powder, and ground almonds. Beat in the eggs, one at a time. Using a spatula, spread the chocolate and almond cream in the uncooked pastry shell until filled halfway. Top with the cooked apple and pear.

To make the crumb topping, rub together all the topping ingredients with your fingertips. Generously spread this over the tart.

Bake in the oven for 45–50 minutes, or until golden. Let cool slightly, then dust with confectioners' sugar and cocoa powder and serve.

Tip

You can use an electric mixer to cream together the butter and sugar mixture in this recipe. Always beat in the eggs one at a time to avoid curdling.

Some combinations are made in heaven, and this is one of the perfect examples—bananas flambéed in dark rum, crunchy buttery pastry, and a rich, warm chocolate ganache.

Warm flambéed banana and chocolate tart

Serves 8
Preparation time: 15 minutes
Cooking time: 20 minutes

7 tablespoons unsalted butter

¼ cup firmly packed light brown sugar

½ cup golden raisins

3 ripe bananas, sliced

2 tablespoons lemon juice

3 tablespoons dark rum

7 oz semisweet dark chocolate, chopped

⅓ cup superfine sugar

3 egg yolks

1 prebaked sweet flaky pastry shell (see page 11), in a 9 inch diameter, 1¼ inch deep tart pan

Put half the butter and the brown sugar in a skillet and place over gentle heat, stirring occasionally, until the mixture becomes nice and golden. Add the golden raisins, bananas, and lemon juice and cook until caramelized. Add the rum and flambé (see tip on page 31). Let cool.

Meanwhile, melt the dark chocolate and remaining butter in a large bowl set over a saucepan of barely simmering water, making sure the surface of the water does not touch the bowl.

Preheat the oven to 325°F.

Put the superfine sugar and egg yolks into another bowl and whisk together until light and fluffy. Using a rubber spatula, gently fold into the chocolate mixture (make sure the chocolate is not too hot). Cover the bottom of the cooked pastry shell with the banana and raisin mixture. Spread the chocolate mixture on top.

Bake in the oven for 12–15 minutes, or until the chocolate ganache is just set but still wobbly. Serve warm with plenty of crème fraîche.

This rich exotic pie is full of delicious flavors. The fluffy vanilla cream topping is a great contrast to the filling.

Banana and rum pie

Serves 8

Preparation time: 15 minutes, plus chilling

Cooking time: 40 minutes

1 stick butter

2 cups crushed graham crackers

3 large ripe bananas, sliced

⅔ cup dark brown sugar

1 teaspoon ground cinnamon

1 teaspoon grated nutmeg

2 eggs

¾ cup plus 2 tablespoons half-and-half

¼ teaspoon coconut extract

3 tablespoons dark rum

1½ cups heavy whipping cream

⅔ cup confectioners' sugar

2 teaspoons vanilla paste or extract

1½ oz dark chocolate, grated

Melt the butter in medium saucepan and add the crushed graham crackers, stirring to coat them well. Press the mixture into a 9 inch diameter shallow pie plate or ovenproof dish, covering the sides, too. Bake in a preheated oven, at 350°F, for 10 minutes, or until fragrant.

Remove the dish from the oven and reduce the oven temperature to 325°F.

Put the banana slices on a sheet of aluminum foil and toss them with the brown sugar and spices, coating them all over. Cover with another sheet of foil, place on a baking sheet, and bake in the oven for 15–20 minutes, or until mushy. Remove from the oven, but leave the oven turned on.

Put the eggs, half-and-half, coconut extract, and rum into a bowl and beat well. Stir in the cooked bananas. Pour this mixture into the pie shell and bake in the oven for 25–30 minutes, or until wobbly. Cool completely in the dish.

Whip the cream, confectioners' sugar, and vanilla to form nice soft peaks. Pile high on top of the pie and sprinkle generously with the grated chocolate. Chill for at least 1 hour before serving.

Tip

The best way to crush cookies and crackers is to put them inside a strong plastic food bag and bash them with a rolling pin.

This delightful tart is a great summer dessert and will bring a touch of the exotic to your lunch or dinner table. I was inspired by my favorite of the British Virgin Islands, Necker.

Papaya and roasted pineapple tart

Serves 8

Preparation time: 25 minutes, plus cooling

Cooking time: 30 minutes

2 queen pineapples (or small pineapples)

2 tablespoons dry unsweetened coconut

½ cup firmly packed light brown sugar

1¾ sticks unsalted butter, softened

2 tablespoons dark rum

1 prebaked sweet flaky pastry shell (see page 11), in a 9 inch diameter, 1¼ inch deep tart pan

1 lime

2 papayas, peeled, seeded, and thickly sliced

freshly grated nutmeg, for dusting

For the crème pâtissière

6 egg yolks

½ cup superfine sugar

3 tablespoons cornstarch

1½ cups milk

1 vanilla bean, split lengthwise

To make the crème pâtissière, whisk together the egg yolks and sugar in a large bowl until pale and fluffy. Add the cornstarch and mix well. Put the milk and vanilla bean into a large saucepan and bring to a boil. Remove the vanilla bean and pour the steeped milk over the egg mixture, whisking all the time. Pour the mixture back into the saucepan and stir over low heat until it comes to a gentle boil. Cook for 2 minutes. Remove from the heat and let cool.

Peel the pineapples and cut into large chunks, removing the core and reserving a few leaves for decoration. Toss the chunks with 1 tablespoon of the dry coconut and the sugar. Place on a baking sheet and roast in a preheated oven, at 350°F, for 25 minutes, or until nice and golden. Let cool.

When the crème pâtissière is cold, beat in the softened butter and rum. Using a spatula, spread into the cooked pastry shell. Cut the lime in half and rub one half around the edge of the pastry, then sprinkle some of the remaining dry coconut over the lime edge— it should stick to the juice.

Toss the papaya with the juice from the remaining lime half and arrange the papaya and pineapple on top of the tart. Decorate with the remaining dry coconut and pineapple leaves, if desired. Just before serving this, I like to grate a little fresh nutmeg over the top.

Tip

Always stir continuously when you make crème pâtissière to keep the mixture smooth.

Saffron has been used in baking for centuries. The sweet taste of this luxurious spice is perfect with the fresh zesty apricots.

Apricot and saffron pies

Makes 6

Preparation time: 20 minutes, plus chilling

Cooking time: 1 hour 20 minutes

butter, for greasing

2 tablespoons all-purpose flour, plus extra for dusting

1 quantity (14½ oz) sweet flaky pastry dough (see page 11)

1 lb 10 oz fresh apricots, halved

½ teaspoons ground cinnamon

4–6 strands of saffron

2 teaspoons vanilla paste or extract

1 cup firmly packed light brown sugar

1 egg, beaten

1 tablespoon superfine sugar

Butter and flour 6 individual 4 inch diameter, 1¾ inch deep springform cake pans. Roll out the dough on a lightly floured surface ⅛ inch thick. Use it to line the pans (see page 18), reserving the trimmings. Chill the pastry shells in the refrigerator for 20 minutes.

Put the apricots, flour, spices, vanilla, and sugar into a large saucepan. Place over medium heat and cook for 10 minutes, or until the sauce is smooth but the apricots are still nice and firm.

Pour the mixture into a strainer, with a bowl underneath to collect the liquid. Arrange the apricots in the pastry shells.

Preheat the oven to 350°F.

Roll out the pastry trimmings and cut out lids, using the pans as a guide. Brush the top edges of the pastry shells with some of the beaten egg. Top with the lids and press and pinch together the edges of the pastry to seal. Brush the tops with the rest of the beaten egg and sprinkle with the superfine sugar.

Cut out 6 small squares of wax paper and roll into cone shapes. Poke one in the top of each pie to act as a funnel for the steam to escape, then bake the pies in the oven for 25–30 minutes, or until golden. Serve with crème fraîche drizzled with the cooking juices from the apricots.

Tip

Always use pure vanilla extract or paste, both of which contain real vanilla, instead of imitation vanilla extract, which is not the real thing.

Sometimes the traditional recipes are the best, and on a cold fall day you can't beat an apple pie—I serve it with hot custard.

Old-fashioned apple pie

Serves 8

Preparation time: 25 minutes

Cooking time: 50 minutes

1 quantity (14½ oz) sweet flaky pastry dough (see page 11)

8 Granny Smith or Cox's apples, peeled, cored, and quartered

grated zest and juice of 2 lemons

¾ cup firmly packed light brown sugar

1 tablespoon all-purpose flour, plus extra for dusting

2 teaspoons ground cinnamon

4 tablespoons slightly salted butter, cut into small cubes, plus extra for greasing

1 egg, beaten

Preheat the oven to 350°F. Grease and flour a 10 inch diameter shallow pie plate.

Divide the dough into 2 pieces, roughly one-third and two-thirds. Roll out the larger piece on a lightly floured surface to ¼ inch thick, and use it to line the pie plate, leaving 2–1–1¼ inches of the pastry overhanging.

Put the apples into a large bowl. Add the lemon zest and juice, sugar, flour, and cinnamon. Using your hands, toss everything about so that the apples are coated all over. Fill the lined pie plate with the apple mixture and dot the butter on top.

Roll out the remaining dough to a circle a little larger than the pie plate. Brush the edges of the pastry shell and lid with some of the beaten egg.

Place the circle of pastry on top of the apples and run the rolling pin around the edge to trim. Using your fingers, pinch the pastry where it joins for a decorative look. Using a cutter or a knife, cut out shapes from the pastry trimmings and stick them on top of the pie with a little beaten egg. Finally, brush the top generously with the rest of the beaten egg. Make a small hole in the center to let the steam escape.

Bake in the oven for 50–60 minutes, or until the pastry is golden and the juices start to ooze out. Serve with hot homemade crème anglaise (see page 169).

Tip

To divide the dough into one-third and two-thirds, first shape it roughly into a flattish square or rectangle. That way it's easy to cut it into three more or less equal parts.

This southern all-American favorite is a great classic. My American friend, chef Art Smith, taught me how to make this recipe, and my friends are addicted to it!

Pecan pie

Serves 8

Preparation time: 10 minutes

Cooking time: 55 minutes

3 tablespoons unsalted butter, plus extra for greasing

1 quantity (14½ oz) sweet flaky pastry dough (see page 11)

all-purpose flour, for dusting

1⅔ cups chopped pecans

1 cup pecan halves

2½ oz semisweet dark chocolate, chopped

3 eggs

1 cup plus 2 tablespoons firmly packed light brown sugar

⅔ cup maple syrup

2 teaspoons vanilla extract

2 teaspoons bourbon whiskey (optional)

Preheat the oven to 350°F. Grease a 9 inch diameter shallow pie plate or tart pan. Roll out the pastry on a lightly floured surface and line the plate or pan (see page 18).

Place the chopped pecans and pecan halves on separate baking sheets and roast them in the oven for about 5 minutes, or until golden and fragrant.

Melt the chocolate and butter in a bowl set it over a saucepan of barely simmering water, making sure the surface of the water does not touch the bowl.

In a separate large bowl, beat the eggs with the sugar, maple syrup, vanilla extract, and bourbon, if using, then beat in the melted chocolate and butter.

Place the chopped pecans in the lined pie plate, cover with the maple and chocolate mixture, and arrange the pecan halves on top.

Bake in the oven for 50 minutes, or until golden and set. Serve warm, with a generous scoop of vanilla ice cream.

Tip

When roasting nuts in the oven, keep an eye on them at all times and don't leave them unattended, because they can burn quickly.

I came across pumpkin pie at my first Thanksgiving celebration, at my dear friends Paul and Laurie's house in LA. I had always thought winter squash, be it pumpkin or butternut squash, was a savory ingredient, but how wrong I was! I have since mastered this recipe and we now sell so many of them at Cake Boy to all our American and British customers.

The BEST pumpkin pie

Serves 8

Preparation time: 15 minutes

Cooking time: 55 minutes, plus 40 minutes for the pumpkin

1 butternut squash (about 2 lb), roasted and pureed (see right), or 2 x (15 oz) cans pumpkin puree

butter, for greasing

about 1 quantity (13 oz) sweet flaky pastry dough (see page 11)

all-purpose flour, for dusting

1 (14 oz) can condensed milk

3 eggs

1 teaspoon ground cinnamon

1 teaspoon ground nutmeg

confectioners' sugar, to dust

You can get pumpkin puree in a can, but I prefer to spend the extra time and trouble cooking my own puree by using butternut squash. To do this, chop a butternut squash into large wedges, remove the seeds, then place the wedges on a baking sheet and roast in a preheated oven, at 350°F, for 40 minutes or until really soft and tender. Scoop out the soft flesh and press it through a strainer—the taste is divine!

Preheat the oven to 325°F. Grease a 12 x 8 inch, 2 inch deep pie plate or ovenproof dish. Roll the dough out thinly on a lightly floured surface and use it to line the dish (see page 18).

In a bowl, mix together all the remaining ingredients until smooth. Fill the pastry shell and bake in the oven for 50–55 minutes, or until set but with a slight wobble in the middle. Let cool in the pie plate.

Dust generously with confectioners' sugar and serve with whipped cream, topped with caramelized pecans.

Tip

If you don't have time to make your own pumpkin puree you can substitute canned pumpkin puree, available in most food stores.

I travel to the United States a lot and I'm a great fan of American baking. The bakeries and farmers' markets there are full of the most beautiful and delicious pies. Blueberry pie is a classic, and, hopefully, my version will match the one from across the pond or be even better.

Blueberry pie

Serves 8
Preparation time: 15 minutes
Cooking time: 40 minutes

butter, for greasing

3½ pints blueberries

1 cup superfine sugar

3 tablespoons cornstarch

2 tablespoons blueberry liqueur (optional)

1⅔ quantities (1½ lb) sweet flaky pastry dough (see page 11)

all-purpose flour, for dusting

1 egg, beaten

Preheat the oven to 350°F. Grease a 10½ x 8 inch, 1¾ inch deep pie plate or ovenproof dish.

Put the blueberries and sugar into a large saucepan and gently heat until the fruits start to soften. Remove a couple of tablespoons of the juices and blend with the cornstarch in a small bowl. Stir the cornstarch into the blueberries and continue to cook over low heat until syrupy. Stir in the liqueur, if using, then remove from the heat and let cool.

Roll out two-thirds of the dough on a lightly floured surface and use it to line the pie plate (see page 18). Fill the pastry shell with the fruit filling. Roll out the remaining dough for a lid. Brush the edges of the pastry shell and lid with some of the beaten egg. Cover the pie with the lid and press and pinch together the edges of the pastry to seal. Trim the excess pastry with a kinife and brush the top generously with the beaten egg. Make a couple of holes in the top for the steam to escape.

Bake in the oven for 35 minutes, or until the pastry is golden and the delicious juices start to escape. Let cool in the dish. Serve with plenty of whipped cream flavored with a little vanilla extract.

Tip

Using cornstarch is a great way to thicken a fruit compote. Just stir a little of the fruit juice into a couple of tablespoons of cornstarch in a small bowl, then stir the mixture back into the fruit.

This spectacular-looking pie (see previous page) is just fabulous. Hiding under the fluffy marshmallow meringue you will discover the exotic flavor of the deep filling.

Exotic fruit meringue pie

Serves 8

Preparation time: 15 minutes, plus chilling

Cooking time: 5 minutes

¼ cup cornstarch

¼ cup all-purpose flour

1¼ cups superfine sugar

⅔ cup lime juice

⅔ cup passion fruit juice

⅔ cup mango puree

2 teaspoons vanilla paste or extract

4 eggs, separated

3 tablespoons unsalted butter

1 prebaked sweet flaky pastry shell (see page 11), in a 9 inch diameter, 1¼ inch deep pie dish

1¼ cups superfine sugar

1 teaspoon cornstarch

Place the flours and sugar in a saucepan and whisk in the juices, mango puree, and vanilla. Add the egg yolks and cook over medium heat for a couple of minutes, stirring continuously, until the mixture thickens. Remove from the heat and whisk in the butter.

Let cool for 10–15 minutes, then pour into the cooked pastry shell. Chill in the refrigerator for at least 1 hour.

Put the egg whites into a large, clean, dry bowl. Using an electric handheld mixer, beat to stiff peaks, adding the sugar and cornstarch alternately, a little at a time. Pile the meringue high on top of the pie, and with a spatula or a flat knife make swirls and peaks. Brown the meringue using a kitchen blowtorch or pass the pie under a hot broiler for 1–2 minutes.

Tip

A kitchen blowtorch is really useful for browning meringue and caramelizing desserts, such as crème brûlée.

There is something very addictive about peanut butter, even more so when it's used as an ingredient. This pie, as well as being fluffy, has the rich addition of chocolate chunks, making it even more luxurious.

Peanut butter and chocolate pie

Serves 8

Preparation time: 15 minutes, plus chilling overnight

Cooking time: 5 minutes

1 cup cream cheese

¾ cup confectioners' sugar, sifted

⅔ cup chunky peanut butter

1 cup heavy whipping cream

1 teaspoon vanilla paste or extract

½ cup semisweet dark chocolate chunks or chips, plus extra to decorate

1 prebaked chocolate flaky pastry shell (see page 12), in a 9 inch diameter, 1¼ inch deep tart pan

light cream, to serve

To decorate

⅓ cup heavy cream

3 oz semisweet dark chocolate, coarsely chopped

1 tablespoon unsalted butter

⅓ cup honey roasted peanuts, chopped

Put the cream cheese and confectioners' sugar into a large bowl and beat together. Beat in the peanut butter.

Beat the whipping cream to nice soft peaks and fold into the peanut butter mixture with the vanilla extract and the chocolate chunks. Fill the cooked pastry shell right to the top, then chill overnight in the refrigerator.

To decorate, melt the chocolate in a large bowl over a saucepan of barely simmering water, making sure the surface of the water does not touch the bowl. Warm the cream in a small saucepan, then pour over the melted chocolate, stirring until nice and smooth. Cut the butter into small cubes, add to the chocolate mixture, and stir until well blended. Let cool slightly.

Drizzle the chocolate topping all over the pie and sprinkle with the roasted peanuts. Serve chilled with cream and grated dark chocolate.

Tip

This chocolate topping is a great way to decorate all kinds of desserts.

Tarte Bourdaloue is a great French classic, and here I am daring to transform the foundations of this recipe into a fabulous pie, adding to it one of my favorite ingredients—preserved ginger.

Pear and ginger frangipane pie

Serves 8

Preparation time: 20 minutes

Cooking time: 1 hour 5 minutes

¾ cup plus 2 tablespoons water

1 vanilla bean, split lengthwise

1½ cups superfine sugar

4 large pears, peeled, cored, and quartered

2½ sticks unsalted butter, softened, plus extra for greasing

3 cups plus 2 tablespoons ground almonds (almond meal)

5 eggs

½ teaspoon almond extract

⅓ cup chopped, drained preserved ginger

1 quantity (14½ oz) sweet flaky pastry dough (see page 11)

all-purpose flour, for dusting

8 oz store-bought or ¼ quantity homemade puff pastry (see page 16)

Bring the water to a boil in a small saucepan. Add the vanilla bean and ¼ cup of the sugar. Reduce the heat, add the pears, and simmer for 10 minutes, or until soft. Remove the pan from the heat and set aside.

Preheat the oven to 350°F. Grease a 12 x 8 inch diameter, 2 inch deep pie plate or ovenproof dish.

In a large bowl, cream the butter, remaining sugar, and the ground almonds until pale and fluffy. Beat in 4 of the eggs, one at a time. Add the almond extract and the ginger. In a separate small bowl, beat the remaining egg and set aside.

Roll out the flaky pastry dough on a lightly floured surface and use it to line the pie plate (see page 18). Brush the edges of the pastry with some of the reserved beaten egg. Spread the almond cream in the pastry shell and push in the drained pears, cut-side down, to cover the pie evenly.

Roll out the puff pastry large enough to cover the pie. Using a lattice roller, cut the pastry and arrange in a lattice pattern over the pie and press and pinch together the edges of the pastry to seal. Trim the excess pastry with a knife and brush the pastry top with the beaten egg.

Bake in the oven for 50–55 minutes, or until golden and puffed up. Serve warm with good vanilla ice cream.

This is my take on the traditional Austrian pastry. Served as a pie, it makes a nice little individual dessert.

Apple strudel pies

Serves 6

Preparation time: 15 minutes

Cooking time: 40 minutes

6 Granny Smith apples, peeled and grated

1⅓ cups firmly packed dark brown sugar

2 teaspoons ground cinnamon

grated zest and juice of 1 lemon

2 tablespoons Calvados, applejack, or brandy

1 cup golden raisins

1 stick unsalted butter, melted

9 sheets of phyllo pastry

2 tablespoons confectioners' sugar

Preheat the oven to 350°F.

Put the apples, sugar, cinnamon, lemon zest, lemon juice, and Calvados into a saucepan and cook for 5 minutes over low to medium heat, until the sugar has dissolved. Stir in the golden raisins, remove the pan from the heat, and set aside.

Butter 6 individual 1¼ cup pie plates or small baking pans, each 4 inch in diameter, 1¼ inch deep. Brush 6 sheets of the phyllo pastry with melted butter and fold each in half to double thickness. Line each pie plate with the folded pastry, letting it overhang the sides. Fill each dish with the apple mixture. Fold the overhanging pastry over the apple filling.

Butter the 3 remaining sheets of phyllo pastry and cut each in half. Scrunch them up and put one on top of each pie.

Bake the pies in the oven for 30 minutes, or until the pastry is crisp and golden. Dust generously with the confectioners' sugar and put back into the oven for another 5 minutes, or until the sugar melts and starts to caramelize. Serve immediately with a light caramel sauce.

Tip

For a quick caramel sauce, put 1 cup superfine sugar in a heavy saucepan over high heat and cook until the sugar is dark golden in color. Remove from the heat and stir in 4 tablespoons unsalted butter. Put back on the heat and slowly stir in 1 cup warmed heavy cream until combined and the sauce thickens. Pass through a metal strainer to catch any undissolved sugar before serving warm.

Traditionally from eastern France, sweet cheese pies are now very popular. They are a mixture between a cheesecake and a pie. This one is made with fresh raspberries which makes it the perfect dessert.

Raspberry cheesecake pie

Serves 9

Preparation time: 15 minutes, plus cooling and chilling

Cooking time: 1 hour

2 tablespoons raspberry preserves

1 prebaked sweet flaky pastry shell (see page 11), in an 8 inch square, 2½ inch deep baking pan or ovenproof dish

3 cups cream cheese

½ cup heavy cream

4 extra-large eggs, beaten

1 cup firmly packed light brown sugar

2 teaspoons vanilla paste or extract

1 tablespoon kirsch

grated zest of 1 lemon

3 tablespoons all-purpose flour

1 tablespoon cornstarch

1¼ cups fresh raspberries

Preheat the oven to 325°F.

Spread the preserves over the bottom of the cooked pastry shell.

In a large bowl, combine the cream cheese with the cream. Beat in the eggs, then the sugar, vanilla, kirsch, and lemon zest. Fold in the flours, then pour the mixture into the pastry shell on top of the preserves. Push the raspberries into the filling.

Bake in the oven for 1 hour, then turn the oven off and let the pie cool inside, with the door ajar. Leave in the pan or dish and place in the refrigerator to set for at least 1 hour before serving. Serve with a generous helping of crème fraîche.

Tip

Cooking the cheesecake filling slowly and letting it cool down inside the oven helps to avoid cracks from appearing on top.

This pie is a real indulgent treat and will become your new favorite chocolate recipe! The combination of the chocolate pastry and the smooth rich chocolate filling makes it irresistible.

Southern chocolate mud pie

Serves 10

Preparation time: 15 minutes, plus chilling

Cooking time: 55 minutes

7 oz semisweet dark chocolate, roughly chopped

1½ sticks unsalted butter, softened

1½ cups firmly packed dark brown sugar

4 extra-large eggs, beaten

¼ cup unsweetened cocoa powder

1⅔ cups heavy cream

2 teaspoons chocolate extract (optional)

1 prebaked chocolate flaky pastry shell (see page 12), in a 10 inch diameter, 2½ inch deep tart pan or ovenproof dish

2 cups heavy whipping cream

3 teaspoons vanilla sugar

2 teaspoons finely grated semisweet dark chocolate

Melt the dark chocolate in a bowl over a saucepan of barely simmering water, making sure the surface of the water does not touch the bowl. Set aside to cool.

Preheat the oven to 325°F.

Cream the butter and sugar until nice and fluffy using an electric handheld mixer or a freestanding mixer. Gradually beat in the eggs, one at a time, on low speed. Sift the cocoa powder over the eggs and stir in, along with the cooled melted chocolate. Stir in the heavy cream and the chocolate extract, if using.

Pour the mixture into the cooked pastry shell and bake in the oven for 45–50 minutes, or until just set. Let cool, then chill in the refrigerator.

Remove from the refrigerator 1 hour before serving. Whip the whipping cream and vanilla sugar to form soft peaks. Pile on the top of the pie and sprinkle with the grated chocolate. Enjoy!

The buildup to the festive season in the UK wouldn't be the same without mince pies, and it's a tradition I was more than happy to embrace—I just love them! I've added a little Italian twist to this recipe ...

Mince pies

Serves 6

Preparation time: 30 minutes, plus marinating

Cooking time: 20 minutes

For the mincemeat

1¾ cups golden raisins

1¼ cups halved candied cherries

1¾ cups raisins

½ cup candied peel

1 stick unsalted butter

1 teaspoon ground cinnamon

1 teaspoon ground nutmeg

1 teaspoon ground allspice

finely grated zest of 1 orange

finely grated zest of 1 lemon

1 cup firmly packed dark brown sugar

1 cup amaretto liqueur

For the pies

butter, for greasing

1 quantity (14½ oz) flaky pastry dough (see page 10)

all-purpose flour, for dusting

8 oz store-bought or ¼ quantity homemade puff pastry (see page 16)

1 egg, lightly beaten

1 tablespoon light brown sugar

The mincemeat should be made a few weeks before you use it for this recipe for the flavors to develop, but trust me—it is worth waiting for.

Put all the dried fruit and spices into a large bowl and mix thoroughly. Place the grated zest, sugar, and amaretto in a small saucepan and heat gently until the sugar has dissolved—do not let it boil. Pour the liquid over the mixed fruit and stir gently, without breaking up the fruits. Cover the bowl with plastic wrap and let steep for 48 hours. Pack the mincemeat into sterilized jars and seal. Store in the refrigerator for up to 2 weeks to let the flavors mature.

When you are ready to make the mince pies, preheat the oven to 350°F. Grease 6 individual 4 inch diameter, loose-bottom tart pans.

Roll out the flaky pastry dough thinly on a lightly floured surface and use to line the pans (see page 18). Generously fill the pastry shells with the mincemeat (this will use approximately 1¾ cups).

Roll out the puff pastry thinly on a lightly floured surface and brush it with the beaten egg. Using a star-shaped cutter, cut out 6 star shapes, or any shape you like, to cover the tart and place them on top of the mincemeat. Sprinkle with the light brown sugar.

Bake in the oven for 25–30 minutes, or until the pastry is golden and the stars have all puffed up. Serve warm with some crème fraîche drizzled with amaretto and sprinkled with roasted slivered almonds ... yum yum!

Tip

This recipe will also make 24 small pies in two 12-hole muffin pans; reduce the cooking time to 20–25 minutes or until the pastry is golden.

When I was growing up we would have a traditional *galette des rois* made with rich almond cream every January to celebrate the Epiphany. This is my all-year-round version, made with sweet apricots and a pistachio cream.

Apricot and pistachio pithivier pie

Serves 8

Preparation time: 25 minutes, plus chilling

Cooking time: 25 minutes

1 stick unsalted butter, softened

¾ cup superfine sugar

1 extra-large egg

1 cup ground pistachio nuts

1 tablespoon all-purpose flour, plus extra for dusting

1 tablespoon kirsch

1½ lb store-bought puff pastry or ¾ quantity homemade puff pastry (see page 16)

2 egg yolks, beaten

½ (15 oz) can apricot halves in syrup, drained

For the syrup

⅓ cup superfine sugar

⅓ cup water

Cream the butter and sugar until light and fluffy. Beat in the egg, then fold in the ground pistachios, flour, and kirsch.

Divide the dough in half and roll out each piece on a lightly floured surface to ¼ inch thick. Cut a 9½ inch circle from one piece and a 10½ inch circle from the other. Place the smaller circle on a baking sheet and brush the inside border with some of the beaten egg yolk. Spread the pistachio cream in the center, leaving a ¾ inch border around the edge.

Cut the apricot halves in half again and arrange them on the pistachio cream. Cover with the larger circle of pastry and press and pinch together the edges of the pastry to seal. Flute the edge by pressing the index and middle fingers onto the pie edge, then make small cuts with a knife between them to create a scalloped edge. Brush all over with the rest of the egg yolk. Score a curved pattern on top with a sharp knife, then let chill and rest in the refrigerator for at least 1 hour.

When you are ready to cook the pie, bake in a preheated oven, at 400°F, for 25–30 minutes, or until risen and golden.

Meanwhile, make a sugar syrup by boiling together the sugar and water for 5 minutes. As soon as the pie comes out of the oven, brush the syrup over the top to give it a lovely glossy finish.

Tip

Brushing the edges of the pastry with beaten egg yolk is really important here—the pastry needs to be firmly sealed so that the filling cannot escape.

1 Divide the pastry in half and roll out each piece.

Apricot and pistachio pithivier pie

2 Cut a 9½ inch circle from one piece and a 10½ inch circle from the other.

5 Fold in the pistachios, flour, and kirsch.

6 Spread over the pastry.

7 Arrange the apricots on top.

3

Transfer the smaller circle to a greased baking sheet and brush the edge with beaten egg yolk.

4

Cream the butter and sugar, then beat in the egg.

8

Cover with the larger pastry circle.

9

Flute the pastry edge, brush with beaten egg yolk, and score a curved pattern on top with a sharp knife. Chill in the refrigerator before baking

I love it when blood oranges are in season. They've got such a different flavor to regular oranges and the color is just divine. They're perfect for beautiful baking. This pie is a great end to a celebratory meal ... and of course you can use regular oranges if blood oranges are out of season.

Caramelized blood orange pie

Serves 8

Preparation time: 15 minutes, plus chilling

Cooking time: 15 minutes

scant ⅔ cup cornstarch

grated zest of 2 oranges

2 cups fresh blood orange juice

1¼ cups superfine sugar

4 egg yolks

1 prebaked sweet flaky pastry shell (see page 11), in a 9 inch diameter, 2½ inch deep pan or ovenproof dish

2 tablespoons warmed, strained apricot preserves, for glazing

For the caramelized orange slices

⅓ cup superfine sugar

⅓ cup water

3 blood oranges, thickly sliced

Put the cornstarch and orange zest into a large bowl and blend in the orange juice.

In a separate bowl, whisk the sugar and egg yolks until pale and fluffy. Stir in the orange juice mixture. Pour the mixture into a heavy saucepan, place over medium heat, and bring to a boil, stirring continuously. Simmer for 2 minutes, stirring until thick. Pour into the cooked pastry shell, let cool, then put into the refrigerator to set for 1 hour.

Meanwhile, make the caramelized orange slices. Preheat the oven to 350°F. Put the sugar and water into a large skillet and bring to a boil, stirring until the sugar has dissolved. Add the orange slices and simmer for 12–15 minutes, turning occasionally, until they have softened and the rind looks almost translucent.

Place the orange slices on a silicone baking mat or a piece of aluminum foil on a baking sheet and bake them in the oven for about 10 minutes, or until they start to caramelize and turn golden but still retain their ruby color. Let them cool, then arrange them on top of the pie and glaze with the apricot preserves.

Tip

There is a season for blood oranges—from Christmas to the beginning of May—so look out for them in the stores during this period if you want to use them for this pie.

This deep pie is very addictive and a perfect winter warmer. When I want to be seriously indulgent, I add semisweet dark chocolate chips, too ... Oops!

Hazelnut bread and butter pudding pie

Serves 8

Preparation time: 15 minutes, plus soaking

Cooking time: 52 minutes

butter, for greasing

about ½ quantity (8 oz) chocolate flaky pastry dough (see page 12)

all-purpose flour, for dusting

6 eggs, lightly beaten

1 brioche loaf

1 cup chocolate and hazelnut spread

1¼ cups milk

1¼ cups heavy cream

½ cup roasted hazelnuts, chopped

½ cup semisweet dark chocolate chips (optional)

¼ cup superfine sugar

Grease a 10½ x 8 inch diameter, 1¾ inch deep pie plate or ovenproof dish. Roll out the dough on a lightly floured surface and use it to line the dish (see page 18). Cover with parchment paper and pie weights or dried beans and prebake in a preheated oven, 350°F, for 15 minutes.

Remove the paper and weights, then use a little of the beaten egg to brush the inside of the pastry shell. Return it to the oven for 2 minutes to seal the pastry.

Slice the brioche thickly and spread each slice with the chocolate and hazelnut spread.

Add the milk and cream to the beaten eggs and whisk.

Layer the brioche, chopped hazelnuts, and chocolate chips, if using, in the pastry shell. Pour the egg mixture over the briocher, fill to the top, and let soak for 10 minutes. Fill with any remaining egg mixture, if necessary.

Sprinkle the sugar on top to create a crust when baking, and bake in the oven for 35–40 minutes, or until golden. Let stand for 10 minutes, then serve with crème anglaise (see page 169).

Tip

Brushing the blind-baked pastry shell with beaten egg forms a seal and makes sure the filling doesn't make the shell soggy.

This is an unusual combination, but trust me—it works very well, and it's a perfect and refreshing palate cleanser. Make sure the mangoes are not too ripe or the fruit will turn mushy.

Mango and green peppercorn pie

Serves 8

Preparation time: 15 minutes

Cooking time: 35 minutes

1 cup milk

1 teaspoon vanilla extract

3 egg yolks

⅓ cup superfine sugar

3 tablespoons cornstarch

3 large mangoes, cubed

1 tablespoon green peppercorns in brine, drained

1 egg, beaten

8 oz store-bought or ¼ quantity homemade puff pastry (see page 16)

all-purpose flour, for dusting

Preheat the oven to 400°F. Grease a 10 inch diameter shallow pie plate.

Put the milk and vanilla extract into a saucepan and bring to a boil.

Mix together the egg yolks, sugar, and cornstarch in a bowl. Pour in a little of the hot milk and stir to blend. Pour the cornstarch mixture into the hot milk in the saucepan and slowly bring back to a boil, stirring continuously. Simmer for 2 minutes, still stirring, until thickened. Cool slightly, then pour into the pie plate.

Mix the mangoes with the peppercorns and place them on top of the custard. Brush the edges of the dish with some of the beaten egg.

Roll out the puff pastry on a lightly floured surface to the size of the pie plate. Cut it with a lattice wheel or into strips and arrange on top of the mangoes in a lattice pattern. Press down well on the edges to stick and brush with the rest of the beaten egg.

Bake in the oven for 30 minutes, or until the pastry is puffed up and golden. Serve warm, on its own.

Quick sweet bakes

Recipe ideas using store-bought pastry dough

Cinnamon sticks serves 4

Mix 3 tablespoons of superfine sugar with 2 teaspoons of ground cinnamon. Brush a sheet of store-bought puff pastry with beaten egg and sprinkle over the cinnamon mix. Cut the pastry into ½ inch wide strips. Twist them, then place on a nonstick baking sheet and bake in a preheated oven, at 350°F, for 7–8 minutes, or until crisp and golden. Perfect for a sweet treat.

Banana and chocolate puffs serves 4

Unroll a sheet of store-bought puff pastry and cut into 4 squares. Place them on a nonstick baking sheet and brush the edges of each square with beaten egg. Spread a tablespoon of chocolate spread in the center of a square and place half a sliced banana on one half, then repeat for the other squares. Fold over the pastry to cover the banana and form a triangle, sealing together the edges well. Brush with beaten egg, then make a few scores across the top of the pastry and sprinkle each one with a little superfine sugar. Bake in a preheated oven, at 350°F, for 10–15 minutes, or until puffed up and golden. Serve warm with scoops of vanilla ice cream.

Rocky road pastries serves 12

Place a sheet of store-bought puff pastry on a nonstick baking sheet. Top with 5 oz of chocolate chunks, 10 broken Oreo cookies, 2¼ cups of miniature marshmallows, and ½ cup of coarsely chopped pecans. Bake in a preheated oven, at 350°F, for 20–25 minutes or until the pastry has cooked. Let cool before cutting into squares.